CULTURAL

STUDIES

Volume 2   Number 1   January 1988

CULTURAL STUDIES is a new international journal, dedicated to the notion that the study of cultural processes, and especially of popular culture, is important, complex, and both theoretically and politically rewarding. It is published three times a year, with issues being edited in rotation from Australia, the UK and the USA, though occasional issues will be edited from elsewhere (e.g. one from Italy in 1988). Its international editorial collective consists of scholars representing the range of the most influential disciplinary and theoretical approaches to cultural studies.

CULTURAL STUDIES will be in the vanguard of developments in the area worldwide, putting academics, researchers, students and practitioners in different countries and from diverse intellectual traditions in touch with each other and each other's work. Its lively international dialogue will take the form not only of scholarly research and discourse, but also of new forms of writing, photo essays, cultural reviews and political interventions.

CULTURAL STUDIES will publish articles on those practices, texts and cultural domains within which the various social groups that constitute a late capitalist society negotiate patterns of power and meaning. It will engage with the interplay between the personal and the political, between strategies of domination and resistance, between meaning systems and social systems.

CULTURAL STUDIES will seek to develop and transform those perspectives which have traditionally informed the field — structuralism and semiotics, Marxism, psychoanalysis and feminism. Theories of discourse, of power, of pleasure and of the institutionalization of meaning are crucial to its enterprise; so too are those which stress the ethnography of culture.

Contributions should be sent to either the General Editor or one of the Associate Editors. They should be in duplicate and should conform to the reference system set out in the Notes for Contributors, available from the Editors or Publishers. They make take the form of articles of about 5000 words, of kites (short, provocative or exploratory pieces) of about 2000 words, or of reviews of books, other cultural texts or events.

Advertisements: Enquiries to David Polley, Methuen & Co Ltd,
11 New Fetter Lane, London EC4P 4EE.

Subscription Rates (calendar year only): UK and rest of the world:
individuals £20; institutions £37; North America: individuals $38;
institutions $60. All rates include postage; air mail rates on application.
Subscriptions to: Subscriptions Department, Methuen & Co Ltd, North
Way, Andover, Hants, SP10 5BE.

Single copies; from above address £14/$28.

ISSN 0950–2386

CONTENTS

MEAGHAN MORRIS

AT HENRY PARKES MOTEL

A motel is a motel anywhere.
(Robert Venturi)

I

BRICK WALL

On the 24th October 1889 Sir Henry Parkes Colonial Secretary and Past Member for Tenterfield made his Historic Federation Speech. As a result of this Speech the Commonwealth of Australia was formed.

The Sydney Mail referred to Sir Henry Parkes as Australia's Most Farsighted Statesman. This Motor Inn is located 180 metres from the Place where that Famous Speech was delivered. It is called 'The Henry Parkes' in Honour of this Great Statesman.

■

There is a Legend inscribed on the street-front wall of the Henry Parkes Motor Inn, Tenterfield.

It tells a story about one of the representative Great Men of colonial New South Wales – an immigrant, self-made man, traveller, poet, journalist, and an indefatigable patriarch in his family and political life – founding the modern nation with a speech act.[1]

It is also the story of a journey famous only for being interrupted in a small rural town. Parkes was returning to Sydney from Brisbane after talks with Queensland leaders, and stopped in Tenterfield to issue a press release (an after-dinner oration). The story of his speech is repeated now to attract the attention of travellers passing through that town today.

I should like to be able to say that a reading of this Legend *in situ* could be a useful starting-point for a feminist essay in cultural studies.

It raises familiar questions about the past represented in the present (myths of nationality, origin, engendering). But it does so in a context formed by everyday cultural activities – driving, stopping at a motel, tourism, small-town life – in which the Legend is used to engender effects of *place*. It attempts to persuade passing tourists to stop, and to define the town to its residents. To thematize relations between past and present, mobility and placement, is the minimal semiotic (promotional) programme of any memorial-motel. The Henry Parkes in this respect is usefully self-reflexive.

A feminist reading might question, for example, whether the myths of national and local history produced in the practices of tourism may also imply, and intersect with, a gendering of the spatio-temporal operations (movement/placement) on which those practices depend.

This is a question about representation: figures (moving) in a landscape. But a feminist reading would also want to invest any motel context with effective political significance. Motels are often used today as privileged sites of a road-runner *Angst* (the *Paris, Texas* model). In that guise, they usually signify a transcendental homelessness. But, with its peculiar function as a place of escape yet a home-away-from-home, the motel can be rewritten as a transit-place for women able to use it. On the one hand, motels have had liberating effects in the history of women's mobility. They can offer increased safety to that figure whom Trollope once described as the Unprotected Female Tourist, and promise decreased bother to women on 'holiday' with their families. On the other hand, they fix new sites of placement for domestic, affective, and sexual labour, paid as well as unpaid.

So the motel can be used to frame and displace, without effacing, the association of men with travel and women with home that organizes so many Australian 'legends' – in academic as well as popular and recycled touristic forms. A memorial-motel is a complex site of production, and one in which conflictual social relations cannot sensibly be ignored.

■

But, if the text of a motel Legend seems to represent a likely point of departure, a tour of recent cultural studies can make it surprisingly hard to get there.

For each direction of research I've mentioned, there is a different kind of objection.

First, there's a problem about what counts as the proper use of *time* in analysis of popular culture. Iain Chambers, for example, declares in *Popular Culture* that, since 'in the end, it is not individual signs, demanding isolated attention, but the resulting connections or "bricolage" – the style, the fashion, the image – that count', we should, in response to popular culture, refrain from resubjecting it to 'the contemplative stare' of 'official culture'. To linger too long at a motel wall, or to 'read' its inscription too closely, requires a tempo inappropriate to my object: such reading 'demands moments of attention that are separated from the run of daily life'.[2] The past-in-the-present is now a look, not a text.

Then there is a problem about *placement*. For Georges Van den Abbeele in 'Sightseers: the tourist as theorist', studious reading does not contradict the daily pursuits of tourism. He sees them as fellow travellers: tourism is already a mode of cultural studies, and a contemplative mode at that. It can involve research, interpretation, and prolonged moments of intense attention. Yet, for him too, there is a trap involved in lingering at an inscription. The Legend of Henry Parkes is what he calls, following Dean MacCannell,[3] a *marker* – a sign constructing a 'sight'. In studying it, both tourist and theorist can be caught up in a metaphysical quest. Each is motivated by desire 'to make present to himself a conceptual schema which would give him immediate access to a certain authenticity (the "real nature" of his object of study)'.[4]

So if I insist to the first objection that the Legend of Parkes is a tourist tale of politics made on the run, and to the second that it marks for critical inspection a (phallo)logocentric myth, from either side this motel wall represents, as an object of reading, a desire to limit movement by constructing a singular place. Here comes a third kind of difficulty. For numerous theorists of travel (Fussell, Baudrillard, Virilio . . .) there is no such 'place' to start with. The trouble with a *motel* as a site of analysis is not the familiar gap between a text (a particular motel-in-place) and reading practices (the multiplicity of its uses). Nor is it the pertinence of talking in this way about a bit of the built environment, or a segment of everyday life. The trouble is that, whatever they may say, motels in fact *demolish* sense-regimes of place, locale, and 'history'. They memorialize only movement, speed, and perpetual circulation.

So the project of reading should retreat, perhaps, and recommence, with a view on the run from the road. This is to follow the line of least resistance, a 'populist' approach – though to depart, in order to arrive, is a time-consuming, place-fixating activity. One reason for pursuing it, though, is that it's the kind of popular practice that motels work to foster. Another is that it lets me discard, *en route*, some encumbrances.

The glimpse

You can see from the highway it's a tempting motel, an obvious place to stop. If you come into town from the south, one surge brings you over the mountain and down a slope to the Motor Inn at the bottom. A radiant promise of SPA POOL SAUNA GYM (and, in these cold climes, CENTRAL HEATING) flares out, day and night, at the delicate moment dividing a long, hard haul from Sydney from an easy cruise into Brisbane. This is the last town before the Queensland border. As a scenic view on the northbound road, the Henry Parkes is perfectly timed.

From the north, the approach is less dramatic. Tenterfield is only the first real town in New South Wales, and you would already have driven through most of it. It's pretty, with willows and old stone buildings, but after some three blocks of deserted main street there's not a great deal to stop for. But there's a long, level view of the Henry Parkes on the other side of the highway. Its design is imposing enough to demand serious attention: verandahs curving grandly around a garden courtyard, white-sashed

Georgian windows, and on the front wall of the nearest wing a large commemorative scroll. Clearly a motel, it might also be a gracious residence; a country resort; a health centre; a historic public building. From this direction, the Henry Parkes suggests serious leisure instead of a night's salvation.

Scan

Personified models of action (the weary itinerant coming to rest, the reflective tourist sampling the country . . .) are commonly produced by travel narratives set in and around motels. Any well-designed motel can cite and mobilize a number of these without 'imposing' any one too explicitly. Indeed, the motel form (or 'chronotope', in Bakhtin's terms) has become so richly mythic in our culture that any one motel anywhere must constrain the possibilities. An amorphous, general motelness can be commercially unconvincing at any price except to connoisseurs of the basic.

It isn't simply a matter of suggesting, for 'high speed comprehension' across vast space,[5] a competitive definition of style (cost, ambience, clientele). Motels are transit-spaces, charged with narrative potential. A motel should promise a scenario, and exactly the one you want: a good night's sleep, a stint of poignant alienation, a clandestine adventure, time off housework, a monastic retreat – promises which need have nothing to do with what anyone subsequently does. Veering off the road and into the drive of any motel setting, we seek shelter, rest, and safety, but we also assess a script (even, or even especially, at the lone motel, in the middle of nowhere, no commercial rivals for miles).

The Henry Parkes is distinguished from its close competition by the sense of a 'complex' it generates. The major rival is straight across the road – the Jumbuck, a Homestead Inn. The familiar 'H' sign for the chain *aficionado* is in thick nailed board, and its woodiness is the single concession, apart from the name, to a code of bush nostalgia. The Jumbuck is aggressively *serial* in theme ('You're Home', wherever you are): the asphalt yard is for parking, no nonsense with stately courtyards; a few routine flowers, no pretentiously landscaped shrubs; and, unusually for a New England motel, no effort at Georgian sashing. The sliding windows are uncompromisingly functional, with mean proportions outlined by the plain aluminium of a hardline, no-frills modernism. The Jumbuck makes minimal use of allusiveness to other building forms. It could be, at best, a raw new home in a brand-name housing settlement. Anywhere else, the same design might merely be motel-basic. But opposite the florid expanse of the Henry Parkes it claims austerity and rigour. The Jumbuck is a real motel, for travellers on serious business.

So the reflective tourist arrives at a scholastic dilemma where Miles Street meets Rouse Street, Tenterfield. On one side of the road, a myth of the Modern Universal: seriality, chain self-reference, territorialization by repetition-and-difference; '*a Homestead is a Homestead everywhere*'. On the other, Postmodern Particularity: *bricolage* individuality-effect, pluralist pastiche coding, localization by simulated aura: *'this motel is The Motel in Tenterfield'*.

In each case, the major signifiers of these myths are equally myths of Australianness (the motel signs: Jumbuck, Henry Parkes) and of Home (the suburban referent of their design). But these function quite differently on either side of the road. The Jumbuck is a national-*identity* synecdoche, as internationalizing in form as a Tudor Inn or a Ten-Gallon Hat; its model of 'home' is a standardized housing. The Henry Parkes, in contrast, advertises *personality*: a locale appropriates a 'historic' name, to claim special regional significance; and the 'home' it offers is a middle-class splendour, customized to connote 'uniqueness'. The Jumbuck is a motel to use, the Henry Parkes a place to visit.

Quandary

On the road, the choice can be quickly reduced to price, availability, mood. So, for some reflective tourists, there could be no choice involved. A motel, by definition, can never be a true *place*: the locality-effect of the Henry Parkes is an optical illusion.

Following an influential distinction derived from Daniel Boorstin, for example, any motel is necessarily one of the 'pseudo-places' defining the tourist world.[6] For Paul Fussell, the characteristic sign of the pseudo-place (from Disneyland to the airport, Switzerland to the shopping centre) is a calculated readability.[7] True places are opaque to the passing observer and 'require' active response (ideally, the rich interpretation that was 'literature' in the lost era of 'travel'). Pseudo-places achieve an artificial transparency, inducing the passivity typical of 'tourism'. It follows that motels juxtaposed in space can only be rival pseudo-places. In Tenterfield (part place, part pseudo-place) the most that could be said is that, while the Jumbuck celebrates its pseudo-place status, the Henry Parkes tries to hide it. The difference is mere variation apprehended in a high-speed, empiricist *flash*. Indeed, the rapidity with which I can 'recognize' the difference is the sign of its pseudo-status.

With its dependence on cultural élitism and on a realist epistemology, the idea of the 'pseudo' has shown a surprising tenacity in recent cultural studies. Jean Baudrillard's concept of hyperreality owes a good deal to Boorstin's work, and can be written back into its terms. In the world of third-order simulacra, the encroaching pseudo-places finally merge to eliminate places entirely. This merger is a founding event: once it has taken place, the true (like the real) begins to be reproduced in the image of the pseudo, which begins to become the true.[8]

In this optic, my two motels can only be 'recognized' as generators of a hyperreal country town. Adjacent features – old houses, paddocks, sheep – become, like 'rural' faces in the street, indifferently either vestiges of the old order of the Real, or simulacra of the old (more true than the true, more rural than the rural) for the new order of hyperreality.

For both Fussell and Baudrillard, the irreality of motels is of an objective order. Both write allegories of subjects in movement halting here and there in an obdurately recognizable landscape: Fussell's tourist requires the known; Baudrillard's theorist always finds it.

Acceleration

A slightly different rejection of the Henry Parkes can be produced by simply not stopping – writing the subject as a zooming observer, tourism as a history of *speed*.

For Paolo Prato and Gianluca Trivero (scanning Fussell's use of Boorstin via the work of Paul Virilio), 'Speed undoes places (events [*faits*] become non-events [*défaits*], Paul Virilio) and a succession of pseudo-places reduces the complexity of the environment to hotel chains, motorway restaurants, service stations, airports, shopping centres, underpasses, etc.'[9] And indeed, for Virilio, speed consumes time, narrative, and subjectivity as well as space: speed is itself a 'non-place', and the users of transit-spaces, transit-towns (like airports), are spectral – 'tenants . . . for a few hours instead of years, their fleeting presence is in proportion to their unreality and to that of the speed of their voyage'.[10]

In the 'accelerated impressionism'[11] of an aesthetics of disappearance, 'the' landscape becomes a blur, a streak, and no sense of place can survive.

But, if there is a spectre haunting transit-space in these racy formulations, it is perhaps the figure of the peasant rather than that of the short-term tenant. Duration, stability, accumulated experience, reality itself are products of relative immobility in a permanent and singular place: which is to say, they are rhetorically immobilized *categories*. They don't really move in history, or transform in response to transit-ion. The founding myth here is not geographic (the progressive encroachment of the pseudo-sphere) but historical: the trauma of humanity's first train ride, the thrill of first contact with cinema.[12] Unlike Baudrillard's hyperrealist, however, the subject of zoom analysis is eternally fixed in her originary moment. Hurtling on in the accelerating placelessness of speed, she's a figure in chronic stasis.

U-turn

However, Paul Virilio's notion of the 'lodgement' as a *'strategic installation'* (establishing 'fixed address' as a monetary and social value in the history of mobilization)[13] allows for slowing the pace. A motel is a type of installation that mediates (in spatial, social, and monetary terms) between a fixed address, or domicile, and, in the legal sense, 'vagrancy'. It performs this function precisely as a transit-place, a fixed address for temporary lodgement.

Furthermore, the installation of any one motel can easily be seen as strategic. There is not only rhetorical competition with neighbours ('address' projected in space) but a conative effort at stopping the traffic over days as well as moments, to slow transients into tourists and divert energy to places (the motel and its vicinity). The aim of a specialist motel like the Henry Parkes is an elaboration on this – an attempt from a small-town highway spot to alter urban maps of significance. The ploy assumes the transience and plasticity, not the fixity, of meanings constructed in space. So to stop to examine such an effort is also to construct a strategic installation: rather than halting for confirmation (collecting theoretical brochures) at exemplary places or performing their disappearance (hypostatizing motion), it places reading transitionally *at* a site, in a process of place invention.

Tour

Highway clichés aside, the Henry Parkes foyer is in fact a place where the 'fixed' and the 'mobile' meet. Adorned with all the conventional signs of tourism and moteldom, it is both a front office to one wing of the motel and a work-space extension to the family home a few steps away on the left – with activity spilling between them.

To a new arrival looking around, the relationships between parts of the complex are hard to stabilize.

Behind the family home (designed to blend with the motel) is a public sports centre with a large and well-equipped gym; and the passage to it from the motel negotiates a garden-with-pool landscaped in suburban 'backyard' styling. Like many motels with a sporting motif, the Henry Parkes can double as an informal community centre: the therapeutic motel function extends into the local leisure economy. So at any moment, and in most of the spaces defining the complex, there is constant intermingling of the 'host' family's domestic life, the social activities of town residents, and the passing diversions of tourists. The motel's solidity as *place* is founded by its flexibility as *frame* for varying practices of space, time – and speed.

This art of motel extension projects rhetorical identity in space in a manner quite different from that analysed by Venturi, Scott Brown, and Izenour for façades on the Las Vegas strip. In those highway-inflected structures, they see a functional distinction between 'front' and 'back' reflected in formal design: 'Regardless of the front, the back of the building is styleless, because the whole is turned towards the front and no one sees the back.'[14] A front/back regionalization model[15] is thus rewritten as a distinction between a surface (persuasive) rhetoric, which varies, and a deep (enabling) grammar, which does not – 'the neutral, systems-motel structures behind . . . survive a succession of facelifts and a series of themes up front'.

The Henry Parkes abandons these distinctions and the fundamentalism they foster. The façade theme is developed, not restricted or deflated, by the intricate regions behind. The country-resort experience begins on the street and runs all the way back to the fence. As a strategic installation, this motel works *against* the codes of highway inflection – and, in fact, against the pull of the highway. It intrudes into the traffic flow to inflect it towards the town.

It is as a small-business 'front', then, that the Henry Parkes effects a rural solution to the problem defined by Venturi. Its production of itself as a 'place' (and of Tenterfield as a tourist setting) isn't simply a logical progression from the dynamics of highway competition but an effort to reverse and exploit the highway's displacing effect on small towns. It is a common device of theme motels in locations of fragile importance, and one that still allows for variation along the lines described by Venturi. Other sports-theme motels, for example, may function primarily as wrenching body-conversion centres, or as exotic health-and-beauty farms. In this case, however, place is produced as a strongly built form of *'residency'*.

Inside the complex, the resident family, visiting locals, and motel guests all share in a pervasive production of 'home'. The Henry Parkes offers locals not only a little work (house and garden) and an inspiring architectural model of the 'beautiful residence', but the raw material ('strangers') for further home-town promotion. The coherence of the Henry Parkes complex is an embracing and durable familialism. The touristic, the neighbourly, and the proprietorial are related not by opposition (mobile/fixed, touristic/everyday, itinerant/domestic) but along a spectrum divided by degrees of duration, intensities of 'staying' (temporary/intermittent/permanent).

Being there

To change the hospitable rhetoric of the Henry Parkes could be a costly and senseless venture. The most removable, renovatable, and ignorable facet of the place is in fact the Legend of its patron personality inscribed on the scroll at the front.

Bannered across a brick wall, curved elegantly around a plaque and bust, is a Legend of a famous Visitor. This is the motel's 'foundation-stone', its anchorage in History – national (the Federation of Australia), regional (the Tenterfield Oration), and personal (the motel's baptism).

For a cursory glance, the ornate script of the Legend and the bronze effect of the bust need do little more than signify period nostalgia. For many tourists, no doubt, there it stops.

Another kind of cursory glance could read, yet again, the disappearance of history in myth. On this wall, the bitter class struggles of the late nineteenth century, the machinations of a fading patriarch still grasping at political influence, the displacement of the Aboriginal people, and so the very history of this town, this *site*, in battles for land, wealth, power, and the right to determine 'Progress'[16] – all, indifferently, are obliterated by a cloying and sentimentalized sign of the past as timeless colonial *style*.

An experienced history-tourist could even defy the anecdotal status of the Legend, and make it an accessory to the motel's familial myth. It was Parkes, after all (reformer and titular founder of housing, health, prison, transport, communications, and education programmes), who married, in 1890, the dream of a white Australia to a nostalgia for Britain as 'home' – casting, in a memorable and much-commemorated form, the Imperial Family legend: *'The crimson thread of kinship'*, his descendants would repeat, *'runs through us all.'*

Yet there's an imbalance between this all-embracing interpretation of the motel myth and the scroll's quite casual position. On the one hand, the

Legend ascribes great powers to the Word (Parkes spoke, and as a result Australia federated) and to the authority of media citation (*The Sydney Mail* creates Parkes's status). On the other hand – who reads it? What powers does a scroll exercise? The cypress trees in front of it grow taller . . . the locals can ignore it, most tourists may not see it, and who has heard now, anyway, of Henry Parkes? It has the power, at best, to send some trade down the road to see the Place of the Oration. Few travellers, one must imagine, can be expected to take their pleasure in knowingly sleeping and eating 180 metres away from a site of enunciation.

Who can say? Who knows about 'the others'? This is one problem that the scroll can raise, with its story of an exemplary figure's fiat. What actions are performed by positing ideal models of a theoretical practice (and speaking position) appropriate to popular culture? The motel gives pause to think about the question. To give pause is the primary function of the motel as motel anywhere. Back in the rooms of this one, there is, in the midst of a comfortable mix of mod-cons and period-effects, strategically installed, under a window beside the TV, that contemplative place – a desk.

II

DOMESTIC PURSUITS

Political philosophy

Under which thimble – quick! if you please –
Under which thimble now are the peas?
Juggle on juggle, all the day long, –
Sir, you are right! – ah no! – you are wrong!

Then it was R, and now it is C^{17}, –
None of your eyes could follow the pea;
How it was smuggled nobody shows,
How it was juggled nobody knows.

Juggle on juggle, day after day,
Life is a struggle, do what we may;
Wait for our next, and then you shall see
Which is the thimble holding the pea.

Juggle on juggle all the day long,
None are quite right, and none are all wrong;
Life is a struggle ever up hill,
Life is a juggle, say what you will!

(*Henry Parkes, 1870*)

(*Of all Parkes's features as a self-made man, few caused more hilarity to critics during and after his lifetime than his untutored efforts at poetry – except perhaps the 'wandering aspirates' that gave his class origins away. He published five volumes of verse, including many poems about the joys of travel, and others about domestic bliss enjoyed at home with his wife.*)

■

In 'Sightseers: the tourist as theorist', Georges Van den Abbeele makes this comment on the kind of itinerary I've just produced:

> The ritualizing and/or institutionalizing of the voyage can also be an attempt to achieve a certain immediacy (of knowledge, of presence) through the realization of a priorly conceived project. One attempts to circumvent the delay in cognition by being there so to speak before one has begun, by preparing an 'ambush' so that when the experience takes place it can be grasped as fully present.[18]

His article is an intricate commentary on Dean MacCannell's book, *The Tourist: A New Theory of the Leisure Class*. MacCannell argues that tourism emerges in a society no longer dependent on alienated labour but on 'alienated leisure', in which 'reality and authenticity are thought to be elsewhere'.[19] Tourism is a quest to find them. But this quest is made impossible by the very structure of modern tourism. It is defined by a 'semiotics of attraction', in which something (the marker) represents a 'sight' to someone (the tourist). Claiming to indicate the sight, the markers delimit and produce it (since without the proliferation of information and itineraries the tourist would not be able to distinguish the 'sight' from its 'surroundings'). Thinking that he is grasping the reality of a different world, the tourist is in fact always reading the signs of tourism – that is, signs of difference.

In Van den Abbeele's gloss on this argument, a tourist does research for his trip, not merely to avoid discomfort in strange places, but to prepare himself, like an assiduous art student (or a pursuant of truth in politics), for *grasping* the eventual authentic 'sight'. So the tourist as autodidact is perpetually involved in producing and reproducing a metaphysics of presence. He hopes to 'ambush' the sight, but he is always already ambushed by the marker–sight relation.

The trap is unavoidable; and, in one sense, it is the inevitability of 'ambush' that is (like the pious moral of Parkes's Cynical philosophy, the 'desk' in my writing on the wall) always already present to Van den Abbeele's argument.

Rather than retrace the path towards it, I want to sidestep to consider the political inflections of the moves by which Tourism and Theory are read as exemplary, parallel instances of a teleological *drive*.[20] It is difficult to do justice in summary to Van den Abbeele's text, not only because of its complexity but because of its shifting relations to the text of *The Tourist*. To simplify, I shall disarm my own ambush by exposing it at the beginning. Van den Abbeele will argue that the totalizing projects of both Tourism and Theory could be displaced by a theoretico-practical Nomadism. I shall read his argument as developing from three major oppositions that he works to deconstruct – *voyage/home, Man/difference, theory/tourism*. They do not function as equivalents of each other, but I shall read each of them as marked by an implicit valorization of the first term as 'masculine' (that is, unmarked human): a valorization which survives the deconstructive move, *and* in doing so enables an elimination of politics from Van den Abbeele's trajectory.

In his reading of MacCannell, Van den Abbeele accepts that a search for 'destination' is endemic to tourism. Doing so allows him to develop a strong analogy between 'tourism' and 'theory' using the classic epistemological metaphor of the voyage. He *also* limits that metaphor's deployment by reading it as a model of narrative structure. The key figures connecting these operations are *home*, or the *domus*, and *domestication*:

> The tourist theorizes because he is already *en route* and caught up in a chaotic, fragmented universe that needs to be domesticated. The very concept of 'the voyage' is this domestication in that it demarcates one's traveling like the Aristotelian plot into a beginning, a middle and an end. In the case of the tourist, the beginning and the end are the same place, 'home'. It is in relation to this home or *domus* then that everything which falls into the middle can be 'domesticated'. (p. 9)

The project of domestication fails, not only because of the gap between marker and sight, but because the tourist's interpretation always 'lags' behind the activity of voyaging. Domestication is an effort to catch up cognitively with the ever-fleeing experience, or the 'motion', of being *en route*. It is thus an attempt to contain and deny the precedence, as well as the excess, of process over structure. The tourist's problem with 'lag' here becomes, I think, a model of a more fundamental dilemma said to define the speaking being.

In this account of the 'circular structure of referentiality', the *domus* really functions as the ultimate ambush awaiting the tourist. As the fixed point to which the tourist's theorizing attempts to refer, the *domus* is not only always receding as the voyage begins (the designation 'home' is an 'eminently retrospective gesture') but will never be the same when the tourist attempts to 'return'. Home has moved on while the tourist moved away, and the tourist returns transformed by the process of 'domesticating' experience elsewhere.

Van den Abbeele's tourist is trapped, of course, not only by his own myth of Presence and by the aporia of his empiricism, but by a literary variant of both – Tristram Shandy's dilemma. His tourist, chasing 'himself' in time, is a doomed but indomitable realist – forever pursuing a pea.

One problem with this account is the place it accords to 'activity', 'effort', and 'labour'. These terms are made operative only for the voyage, not for 'home' (the elusive ideal that motivates the journey). The *domus* is not reciprocally constructed as a site of work, theoretical or otherwise. Van den Abbeele is quite attentive to the significance of practical activities in tourism (boarding planes, checking in baggage, taking taxis, getting out of bed . . .), but it is strictly, as the ordering of this list suggests, in relation to the rituals of arrival and departure that extend the 'voyage' into the domestic space and make its beginning impossible to fix. That is to say, 'home' is at once a space which is *blank* (so, impossible) and a site of recessiveness: the voyage intrudes into the home, not vice versa (except as a dream of nostalgia). The *domus*, therefore, is figuratively constructed not only as a womb, but as unproductive – a womb prior to labour.

Furthermore, if the work of tourism (research, reading the markers, theorizing the voyage) is a 'domestication', it is because the domestic is understood in the romantic sense of a 'taming' and a 'naturalization'. There is no necessary logical connection between the concepts of coherence and unity (which the tourist tries to impose on a 'chaotic and fragmented universe') and those of home and womb (between which, again, there is no necessary connection). But, of course, there is a very powerful cultural link – one particularly dear to a masculinist tradition inscribing 'home' as the site both of frustrating containment (home as dull) and of truth to be rediscovered (home as real). The stifling home is the place from which the voyage begins and to which, in the end, it returns.

An extreme version may be read in Sam Shepard's *Motel Chronicles*. On the left-hand page, a poem: the world-weary drifter declares, in a moment of 'domesticating' his experiences while not-at-home, 'I've about seen / all the nose jobs capped teeth and silly-cone tits I can handle / I'm heading back to my natural woman'.[21] On the right, a photograph of a woman in a house or motel laundry – her body balanced beautifully between the ironing board and the washing machine. Shepard, in this instance, is the more rigorous theorist of the *domus*. Labour is inscribed on both sides: Man on voyage (writing poem) positions Woman in *domus* (with washing).

In Van den Abbeele's text, the restriction of work to the voyage prevents this sort of crudity from emerging in his schema. It also blocks reflection on the schema's cultural history; it defines, for him, a purely epistemological problem ('the metaphorics of the voyage'). A feminist reading might ask, therefore, what happens to that problem (and the voyage/*domus* opposition) if 'home', rather than the voyage, is rewritten as chaos and fragmentation, labour, transience, 'lag' – or in quite different terms, since these remain a bit too parasitic on the voyage.

But in Van den Abbeele's text the possibility of rewriting 'home' cannot emerge any more than a feminist desire to do so does. The tourist leaving and returning to the blank space of the *domus* is, and will remain, a sexually in-different 'him'.

MAN/DIFFERENCE

One reason for this blankness is that Van den Abbeele follows Dean MacCannell at least some way towards displacing the 'working class' with the 'new leisure class' (of tourists) as a privileged site for analysing modernity. MacCannell considers 'work' used as a tourist spectacle (work displays) to be the very definition of 'alienated leisure' (we work to tour other people working). In Van den Abbeele's text, non-theoretical work drops from sight: the elision of work from the *domus* simply follows from accepting that the tourist's social 'home' is a society of alienated leisure.[22]

Another reason for it is that he goes further than MacCannell in theorizing tourism (and thus 'modernity') as a production of differences, and spectacles of difference. This requires a digression to look at *The Tourist* in more detail.

MacCannell argues that, rather than being organized by simple dualities (such as capital/labour, men/women), modernization is an institutionalized process of 'social structural differentiation'. This means 'the totality of differences between social classes, life-styles, racial and ethnic groups, age grades . . . political and professional groups and the mythic representation of the past to the present' (p. 11). In his version of this by now familiar diagnosis of the post-industrial condition, MacCannell sees differentiation as the 'primary ground' of the feeling of freedom, and also of contradiction, conflict, and alienation, in modern society. Tourism rests on this ground, as a 'collective striving' to transcend differentiation and discontinuous experience by grasping the Big Picture. The tourist as alienated but active cultural 'producer' is thus, for MacCannell, a model of *modern*-man-in-general (p. 1).

This is also why the tourist, for MacCannell, always remains an ambivalent figure. On the one hand, '*sightseeing is a ritual performed to the differentiations of society*' (p. 13). Seeking signs of authentic difference elsewhere, the tourist carries modernization further afield (imperialism). His quest is foiled not only because tourist attractions have the same structure as the differentiations of modern society, but by the effects of his own action in spreading the 'totalizing idea' of modernity. Tourism correspondingly helps to secure a 'strong society' at home; therefore, it may be fundamentally conservative, as well as destructive in the field of modernity's Others.

On the other hand, the quest at least implies a discontent with 'home' (modernity). The issue is complicated by the fact that, while defining the quest as doomed, MacCannell also wants to reject denigration of tourist activity as *in*authentic. It's a matter not just of sympathy for popular culture, but of arguing that the 'rhetoric of moral superiority' to tourism is (especially in the form of touristic anti-tourism) in perfect conformity with the logic of differentiation that motivates tourism. Anti-tourism (contempt for 'the others') is not an analytical reflection on tourism but 'part of the problem' (pp. 10–11).

So the rehabilitation of the tourist is also achieved by suggesting that the tourist may, through his interpretative labour, have an experience of something *like* 'authenticity'. Unlike Paul Fussell, the tourist doesn't find his motels and sights and souvenir shops to be 'pseudo' but enjoys them and keeps on going. He helps to sustain 'a collective agreement that reality and truth exist somewhere in society, and that we ought to be trying to find them and refine them' (p. 155). He is, in his way, a social theorist.

It is only at the last step that Van den Abbeele parts company with MacCannell. He places much greater stress on differentiation as 'the marking process' in tourism – which he radicalizes, in a formalist move, as the '*actual production*' of social differences, rather than the ritual performance of them (p. 10). He also points out that MacCannell's concept of 'social structural differentiation' does nothing to modify the totalizing impulse of theory (or tourism), since 'nothing is so totalizing as a concept of differentiation – nor so apt to be undermined by the very play of differences it attempts to name and de-limit' (p. 13).

The tourist never attains an approximation, or even an intimation, of authenticity, but produces social reality as a kind of 'figural displacement'. It follows that a 'radical politics' of tourism will mean actively affirming the 'supplemental play' of the 'inauthentic' marker, rather than trying to grasp the Sight (or insist on difference). That is to say, the radical tourist will not struggle for transcendence and the refinement of social realities, but will deconstruct his theoretical practice as tourist.

At first sight, it seems that Van den Abbeele's move should lead to a deconstructing of the figure of modern-man-in-general (Man). In fact, something different happens. MacCannell's Man acts out the logic of social-structural differentiation to which, and of which, he is Subject. That is, 'he' is always already socially differentiated (by sex, age, lifestyle, etc.) as a cultural producer, and may be uncomfortable about it. His Manhood, then, is both a grammatical fiction and an unachievable ideal. Van den Abbeele's tourist is an indifferent producer of social reality *as* differentiation: his discomforts emerge not from his own social positioning in difference but from his philosophical mistakes (seeking authenticity, difference). His Manhood, then, is not an object of struggle – something to be achieved – but a presupposition. It still remains the *a priori* of the voyage.

THEORY/TOURISM

If the tourist, for MacCannell, is a social theorist, he is a 'primitive' one – he is 'mystified' about his role in constructing modernity, and his work historically precedes that of the social theorist: 'Our first apprehension of modern civilization . . . emerges in the mind of the tourist' (p. 1). But he has a responsive potential, because of his own discontent. So, for MacCannell, some resolution of the problems posed by tourism may be achieved if social theorists rethink and develop it as a mode of 'community planning'.

Van den Abbeele recoils from both the prospect of 'planning' and MacCannell's claim that his theory of tourism can serve as a theory of social totality. Quite reasonably, he points out that it is really a theory of travel (of modernity seen as 'a perpetual narrative of adventure' (p. 11)), and turns instead to question the politics of producing such an 'all-encompassing' theory. For Van den Abbeele, what is finally at stake is 'less the ideology of tourism than the ideological function of theory' (p. 11).

He takes issue with what he sees as MacCannell's eventual reassertion of the 'superiority' of the social theorist over the tourist. By giving up his radical 'sympathy' for tourism, MacCannell not only reasserts the power of his own position as theorist but repeats the very *gestures* of mystified tourism. Both tourist and theorist attempt to ambush Presence. But the theorist has the greater pretension. He wants to be not just a sightseer but a *seer* – a prophet, in possession of knowledge superior to that of 'the others'. The circle closes: for Van den Abbeele, the theorist, even more than the tourist, is 'part of the problem'.

But whose problem? MacCannell's critique of anti-tourism is based not only on sympathy for the tourist (rejection of élitism) but on a concern for the social consequences of modernity's 'adventure' for the places and people *toured*. It is because of this concern that MacCannell returns in the end to the question of planning. His final position is not simply one of theorist differentiated *from* tourist but of theorist potentially working *with* particular communities planning to be toured. His position as 'seer', then, is more limited in its pretensions than Van den Abbeele can allow.

The 'toured' in fact disappear from Van den Abbeele's account as soon as he introduces his critique of the concept of *totality*. Oddly enough, this happens just as he points out that 'not everyone has either the political right or the economic means to travel' (p. 11), and that MacCannell's theory therefore only deals strictly with the 'leisure class' rather than society as a whole. Van den Abbeele then suggests that, if travel is 'relatively restricted, it must be because of some danger it poses to society's integrity'. This is consistent with his own desire to argue that the excess of the voyage can constitute a threat to the *domus*. But, surely, one might draw the opposite conclusion: if for some societies travel is relatively *unrestricted* for large numbers of people, it is because for the 'home' society it does *not* pose much of a danger to its integrity.[23] This is, of course, exactly why MacCannell sees the 'international middle class' as a problem in the first place.

For Van den Abbeele, however, sympathy for the tourist combined with a critique of totality implies a general transformation of theoretical practice. He proposes a politics of theory in which the excess of the theoretical voyage would not be restrained – and in which the process of theorizing would not attempt to refer back to a *fixed*, 'theorist's', place in a *fixed* society. It is the very presupposition of a fixed position – or *domus* – that must be questioned.

This familiar, indeed 'domestic', conclusion to a deconstructive analysis of the politics of theory then provides a figure to supplant both the Tourist as realist/empiricist/metaphysician of Presence and the Theorist as totalizing Seer. It is the Nomad – who 'renders impertinent' any opposition between rest and motion, between home and travel (p. 13). Invoking Deleuze to insist that the nomad isn't necessarily in motion but can travel '*sur place*', Van den Abbeele speculates that nomadic theory would 'travel from inauthentic marker to inauthentic marker without feeling the need to possess the authentic sight by totalizing the markers into a universal and unmediated vision' (p. 14).

It's a satisfying conclusion, from which it's hard to dissent. The trouble is that, where MacCannell's totalizing concept of modernity does allow for a critique of 'present' social differentiation and for a disarticulation of modern-man-in-general itself by modernity's various Others at home and abroad (precisely because difference is so 'apt to be undermined' by the play it attempts to de-limit), Van den Abbeele's philosophically more sensitive trajectory has the opposite result. It erases social, political, and perhaps theoretical struggle altogether.

In 'Feminist politics: what's home got to do with it?' Biddy Martin and Chandra Talpade Mohanty argue that there can be political limitations to 'vigilante attacks on humanist beliefs in "man" and Absolute Knowledge wherever they appear', if these deny the critic's own situatedness in the social, and in an institutional 'home'.[24] Something like this has happened in 'Sightseers: the tourist as theorist' when, at the end of the road, we are ambushed by a figure who, erasing both the *domus* and difference (therefore becoming, in a sense, autogenetic), and marking a positive denial of situatedness in the social, might well be effectively a model for (post)modern-Man-in-general.

(continued on p. 29)

The Tourist as Theorist 1: (theory takes a holiday)

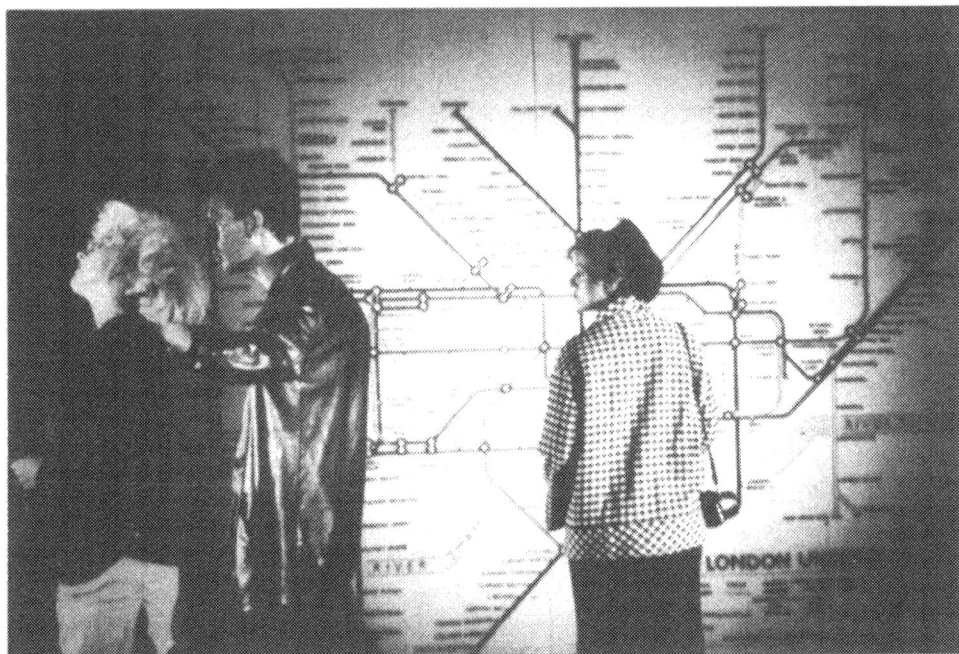

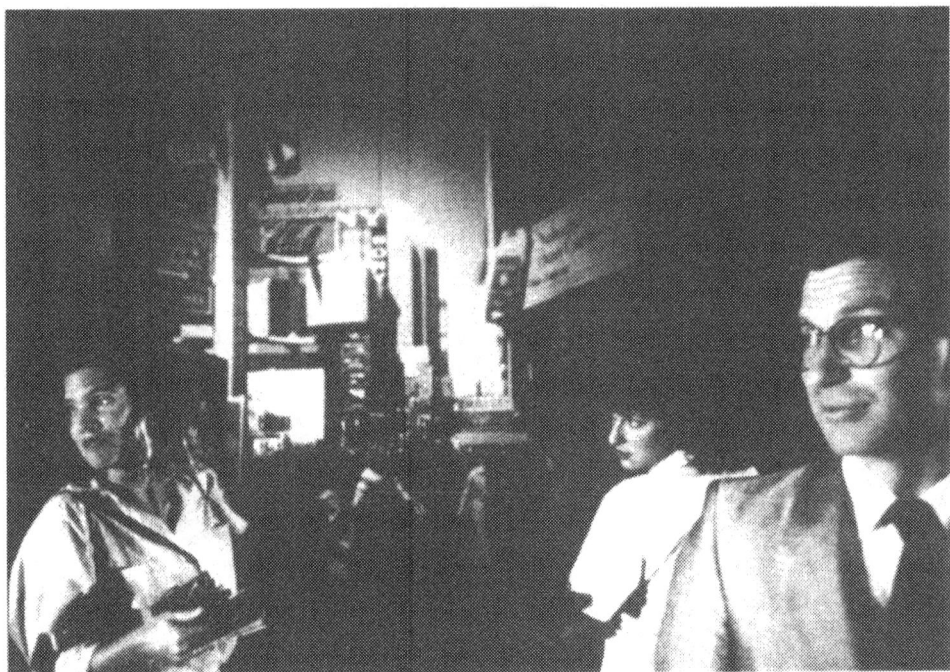

Original Cibachrome prints

Anne Zahalka
1985

28

DOMESTIC PURSUITS (continued)

'Tis misconception all

A PHILOSOPHER said, 'All the world is mad, I am the only sane man in it.'

*   *   *

"'Tis misconception all. The world is mad,
And I alone am sane.' Such the words
Of England's living sage, he rightly proud
Of wisdom in the courts of wisdom.

An unit in that full and flowing crowd
Of miserable maniacs, I, like them,
Was too intent to win the happiness
And worth of life, to value high the search
For possibilities, convertible,
It might be, to the probable. Too full,
Within the limits of a biassed mind,
Of the sweet claims of many clinging friends,
And the dear wisdom of kind deeds,
The daily earnestness of common life,
To yield, unquestioned, that high-voiced demand
Of all-engrossing sanity. Wise, thought I,
Mothers who bend o'er the helpless babes;
And wise the husbandman, who brings
From God's right hand our daily bread;
And wise the toiler 'midst the clang
Of mighty engines for the world's behoof;
And wise, most humbly wise, the innocent,
If ignorant, who bend the knee
And bow the heart to learn of God.
Thus, tho' yet in love with wisdom, I
Shrank back with thoughts akin to hate or scorn,
And called the wise man – egotist.

(Menie Parkes, 1866)

(It's a bit hard to like Menie Parkes, although she is the brilliant daughter effaced by the father's Legend. She had a sad life, and found ferocious consolations in religion. She was Parkes's companion and counsellor, made money writing romances, and married a clergyman who soon died in a fall from a horse. Her own book of poetry was printed privately, as a Christmas gift to her father.)[25]

∎

In 'Maps for the metropolis: a possible guide to the present',[26] Iain Chambers discusses travelling in terms quite different from those of Georges Van den Abbeele. But Chambers also suggests a figure of the modern intellectual, though one with more limited scope for movement and of more focused pursuits than the Nomad – the 'humble detective'.

But if the detective himself is humble, he works a grandiose territory. He cruises through everyday life in a place subsuming both the voyage and the *domus* – the city or, more accurately, the Metropolis (for Chambers, 'the modern world'). Not surprisingly, then, he travels a lot: 'A critical intelligence adequate to the fluid complexity of the present is forced to fly regularly' (p. 5). But eventually 'we also go home'.

The privileged metaphor for Chambers's argument is not the voyage but the *map*. Critical movement is defined not in relation to the temporal 'lag' that fascinates Van den Abbeele, but in relation to spatial shifts between 'perspectives'. There are two major and apparently conflicting ways of mapping the modern world: the *overview* (the theoretical view from the aeroplane – rarefied atmosphere, vast generalization, flat earth as disappearing referent, possible implosion under pressure) and the *close-up* (the view on the ground – 'down-to-earth' observation, local detail, stubborn and violent materiality of terrain, an overwhelming mess of complexities). A working mediation of these two perspectives is possible, however, on the 'giant screen' of the contemporary city. The streaming images of everyday life provide a fluid space of 'immediacy' between the extraterrestrial perspectives of postmodernism and the terrestrial prospects of lived popular culture – while maintaining a tension between the two in 'the semiotic blur' of the Present.

So, where Van den Abbeele's deconstruction of the temporal paradoxes of the travel story finally restructures his map of space (no more tour, no more *domus*), Chambers's mapping of perspectives for remapping space eventually generates a 'guide' to *time* – the empire of the Now, the Contemporary, the Present.

These two projects diverge in a number of ways, which make it difficult for a detective to compare them. One is about tourism, the other about everyday life (though, with their discussions of travel and flight, they overlap). One is situated institutionally by literary theory, the other by cultural studies: while one uses the Aristotelian plot as a trope to define its object, the other refers to punk. One situates itself historically by invoking a 'global' European tradition (the 'metaphorics of the voyage'), the other situates itself in a history of post-war British subcultures. One is an academic reading of a reading, relentlessly contemplative – and so emerges from what Chambers would call 'official culture'. The other scans a mixture of materials with the casual attention characteristic, for Chambers, of 'popular epistemology'.[27] (And there is another difference: Van den Abbeele's text does not make this kind of upstairs/downstairs class distinction, and so provides no counter-accusation to situate Chambers's project.)

In the casually contemplative spirit fostered by a room in a quiet motel, it's also fair to say that, while one is very hard-going, the other is an irresistibly amusing read. Both texts are serious, but one is arduous, like homework, the other fun, like a magazine. It's not just a matter of marking different desires for audience. Van den Abbeele does not, and of course cannot, attempt the 'theorizing without theory' he dreams of for the Nomad. He is searching for the possible, convertible – *it might be* – to the probable. Chambers's detective has no time for postponing the conversion: he writes of the daily earnestness and pleasure of common life, in the now codified pop-theory style that has become a contemporary, informal equivalent of traditional socialist realism.

So it seems in overview. But in close-up there are some interesting points of convergence in the trajectories of the Nomad and the Detective.

Both Van den Abbeele and Chambers establish their topics *territorially*, by a move of metonymic expansion. For the former, the ordinary tourist as social practitioner becomes the Tourist/Theorist as exemplary interpreter, before being transfigured and redeemed as the Nomad. In Chambers's text, expansion operates at the level of a field of action, rather than that of the actor's competence: post-war British (sub)culture becomes 'popular culture' which occupies the Metropolis which becomes co-extensive with 'the modern world', and with the Present. It's not a bad achievement for two moves towards affirming a logic of the local, the limited, the partial, the heterogeneous.

At the same time, both texts insist that the point of departure for such expansion *anticipates*, as well as preceding in practice, its conclusion. Van den Abbeele reclaims MacCannell's thesis of 'the tourist's anteriority to the social theorist' (p. 12) in order to make the Tourist prefigure the Nomad – by providing the structure of the dilemma which the latter must displace. Chambers overtly claims that the metropolitan cultures of the last twenty years have 'fundamentally anticipated' the 'intellectualizing' of post-modernism (pp. 5–7). So, in each case, it is the terrain of everyday life (lived tourist 'theorizing', for Van den Abbeele; cultural 'mixing', for Chambers) that anticipates a general theoretical programme and its actantial 'hero' (Nomad, Detective).

That is to say, the social in each case is inscribed as prophetic of the theoretical conclusion to which each of these texts will come. And in each case that conclusion will assert the displacement of the intellectual as 'prophet'. As the Nomad displaces the seer, so for Chambers the Detective replaces the intellectual 'as a dispenser of the Law and Authority, the Romantic poet-priest-prophet' (p. 20).

At this point, it may appear that a point of departure is emerging, not from the messy complexity of metropolitan culture or the prophetic space of lived theorizing *en voyage*, but from a bibliography of critical writings from the past twenty years – a point of departure retrieved as the ambush of conclusion, recycled, for ritual revisiting, as a *destination* that is inevitable, like the Eiffel Tower, on a tour of present possibilities (or politico-theoretical *markers*). Like Anne Zahalka's photographer ('The Tourist as Theorist'), we begin our planning from brochures and conclude with a review of our personalized images of the sights we set out to see.

When 'Theory takes a holiday', however, the interesting thing is not the reiterations of narrative structure but the re-emergence of a form of personification allegory to articulate that structure. For both Chambers and

Van den Abbeele (unlike Zahalka), 'Theory' not only becomes the subject of the story of flight and transformation but divides, *in the end*, into two figures. The story is remotivated (for future development) by the splitting (and doubling) of Theory into good and bad characters – the Nomad versus the Seer, the Detective versus the Poet-Priest-Prophet.

In his classic study *Allegory: The Theory of a Symbolic Mode*, Angus Fletcher argued that the hero of personification allegory is above all a 'generator of other secondary personalities, which are partial aspects of himself'.[28] The traveller is a 'natural' conceptual hero for such allegory because he is 'plausibly led into numerous fresh situations, where it seems likely that new aspects of himself may be turned up' (pp. 36–7). Following this, the *tourist* would be a likely hero today precisely because he is plausibly led into *familiar* situations, where old aspects of himself may turn up for renewed recycling. Either way, the point for Fletcher is that the splitting-off of 'chips of composite character' is part of a progressive process of reduction that he calls 'daemonic constriction in thematic actions' (p. 38). The daemons of ancient myth share with allegorical agents, says Fletcher, the characteristic of *compartmentalizing function* (p. 40).

Thus, as the Theorist splits into the Nomad and the Seer, the Intellectual into the Detective and the Poet-Priest-Prophet, two diverging daemonic programmes emerge for further adventures by Theory. As the field of action of the hero expands (the nomad universe, the 'modern world'), so, correspondingly, his semantic function is reduced, condensed, and sealed off from that of his necessary Alter Ego.

If this is an odd outcome from what starts out in each case as an affirmation of the priority of complex social experience over totalizing theoretical activity, it is particularly odd as an outcome for Iain Chambers, for whom '*the metaphysical adventure is over*' (p. 20; my italics). This is the claim that enables his displacement of the metaphorics of the voyage with that of the map. If the detective is certainly still an adventurer, he is, as ten thousand screen stories in the naked city have taught us, nothing if not pragmatic about the process of getting results, and the places where he goes to get them. The real mystery in this case is why, if the metaphysical adventure *is* over, the streetwise intellectual should begin his practice so strictly positioned in a constitutive opposition to 'the Other' – particularly since Chambers, like MacCannell, sees a weak sense of detailed differences (the 'others') replacing singular opposition.

But a binary value-system is probably as indispensable to the rhetoric of populism as the construction of emblematic tableaux of personae performing the functions that define them is to its social portraiture. Menie Parkes's scenes of mother with child, husbandman with bread, or toiler with engine can easily be read as prefigurations of Chambers's post-Rasta black Britons with Italian tracksuits and male gender-benders with falsettos – with the difference that Parkes's tableau assumes an eternal congruence of person and persona, while populism today predicates its pedagogy on their radical dissociation. In this sense, and in spite of its anti-academic or anti-'official' stance, populism may well be one political trajectory for which the metaphysical adventure can *never* be over.

One could conclude that if the rhetoric of touristic anti-tourism defines 'part of the problem' rather than a critical perspective, then in a comparable way an academic anti-academicism defines not a transformed politics of theory, but 'part of the problem'. But this formulation is misleading, in that (like the allegory it analyses) it assumes that anywhere and everywhere the problem of 'Theory' is the same. Not the least of the little imperialisms performed by these exercises is to place 'the modern world' as having-been or still-being under the sway of an intellectual Prophet-Despot who sounds for all the world like an elderly humanities professor in a venerable but declining European university.

'The problem' for me is the function performed by the figure of the Prophet ('the Other'), not in the history of the world, but in Iain Chambers's argument. Its main role seems to be to eliminate the difficulties raised fleetingly by Chambers as 'the relationship between . . . the machinery of capital, commerce and industry and ART or CULTURE' (p. 17).

Chambers reasonably points out that these distinctions are highly artificial and promote complacent myths of critical exteriority to culture, and that the 'struggle for sense' occurs inside the powers of the field mutually constructed by 'commerce' and (in his example) music. He argues for situating struggle in the complex 'immediate mishmash of the everyday', rather than in relation to a singular *or* 'free-floating' first cause.

However, in a move which has become increasingly common in recent cultural studies, Chambers immediately retreats from extending the principle of complexity to the problems of relations between the (global) 'machinery of capital' and (local) cultural machinations. Instead of entering the 'field' supposedly constructed 'mutually' by industry and culture, the former simply drops out of play. Put baldly, the result is that 'the immediate mishmash of the everyday' in this account still does not include rapidly changing experiences of the workplace, the home, family life, or mechanisms of state – because it does not include these at all. It certainly does not extend to any flickers of experience of the complexity of relations between high-tech culture and the international, and increasingly internationalized, division of labour that Richard Gordon has called the 'homework economy'.[29]

Instead, as an account primarily (and avowedly) based on the emblematic street experience of un- or under-employed males in European or American cities (or what then becomes its echoes elsewhere), it *restricts* the scope of enquiry to what may well be, in a grim sense, one of the 'growth' areas of that economy – but which does not necessarily thereby serve as a useful synecdoche from which general principles of 'culture' in 'the modern world' may be composed. Perhaps this is one reason why women, in post-subcultural accounts, still appear in apologetic parentheses or as 'catching up' on the streets when they're not left looking out of the window.[30] The ways in which economic and technological changes in 'the 1980s' (in Chambers's phrase) have been transforming women's lives simply cannot be considered – leaving them not so much neglected in cultural studies as anachronistically mis-placed.

Left as a restricted account of local developments, Chambers's 'possible guide' would have a different (more 'modest') force. It's the allegorical expansion that gives the lie, like the myth of the Metropolis, to the rhetoric of the local in Chambers's text, and to many accounts of popular culture which read the collapse of old dichotomies (production/consumption, industry/culture) as an occasion for simply effacing the first term and expanding the second (and most of its traditional content – pleasure, leisure, play, resistance). Yet it's a difficult reading to argue against, precisely because the imaginary figure of the Enlightenment Intellectual – prophet of Truth, poet of Totality, priest of a General Theory, and so on – is still so powerful in debate about culture that the Oedipal effort against him automatically resumes in response to suggestions that relations of production and reproduction, too, are now transformed and transforming in the mishmash of the everyday.

This is precisely how, and why, the figure of the Prophet appears in 'Maps for the metropolis'. After raising the question of relations between industry and culture, and stressing the ambiguities and multiplicities of the 'mix', Chambers immediately rephrases the issue, in straight and simple terms, as one of intellectual 'hostility' to popular culture. Like Van den Abbeele reducing the problem of tourism to sympathy for or against, Chambers shrinks (and moralizes) any critique of capitalism to 'talk of commerce and *corruption*' (p. 20; my italics) – and discovers that behind intellectual 'distaste' for popular culture there is 'a deeper drama. A certain intellectual formation is discovering that it is losing its grip on the world.'

This seems to me to be a nostalgic retreat – not least from the possibility of imagining that the 'deep' drama of anybody's anxieties today may have more generous and urgent resonances than a fear of loss of 'grip' (the intellectual as egotist). It's a retreat from the difficulties that follow once criticism of popular culture is already based on complex experiences of *taste* rather than distaste, of involvement rather than distance, so that a strategic 'siding' for or against the 'popular' becomes a quite pointless manoeuvre. Above all, it's a retreat from asking whether the humanist formation exemplified by the Romantic Prophet has not long ago lost out anyway to that quite different formation which Donna Haraway calls 'the informatics of domination',[31] of which the privileged figure might be (to maintain the allegorical imperative) that exemplary localist, the Stress-Management Consultant – from whose 'daemonic' programme it is not always so easy to differentiate one's own as Other.

Installed in the assiduously stress-free environment of a family-theme motel, the Unprotected Female Tourist tidies her papers, stares at other people's children tumbling past the window on their way to the pool, and wonders whether the woman changing the bedclothes was a girl she went to school with. A feminist, she thinks uncomfortably, should really begin her 'voyage' from these familiar homely markers on the map of everyday life – rather than by chasing, like some raddled detective, the traces of their effacement from the itineraries of 'the others'.

But that's the trouble with travel stories written as Voyages and Maps. They relentlessly generate models of the proper use of place and time – where to begin, where to go, what to become in between. Among the most prescriptive of genres in the canon of modern realism (including 'speculative fiction'), the travel story seems strongly resistant to precisely the effort of transformation that 'Sightseers: the tourist as theorist' and 'Maps for the metropolis' desire to see accomplished.

In Frank Moorhouse's *Room Service* (a useful counter-text to Shepard's *Motel Chronicles*), a story called 'The anti-art of travel' demonstrates the difficulty of overcoming generic models of teleological drive. François Blase – a journalist and tourist who likes to 'rove the world in an inconclusive state' – is confronted in the bar of the Albuquerque Holiday Inn by one of his literary 'others', the Systematic Traveller. In the course of a chat, Blase is harassed by the ST for an account of his theory of travel. Blase resists, but cannot avoid altogether the ambush of reaching a conclusion:

> 'But how do you get a picture of the places you've been to?' the ST said, harriedly.
>
> 'I don't,' I said glumly, 'I just don't. I can't generalize, that's my problem. I can't wrap up my observations in a dazzling conclusive verbal sachet. After all, travel is a damned expensive way to arrive at inconclusiveness . . .'[32]

He hurries on past, however – eventually to end in mid-sentence, muttering inconclusive comments about Boswell and street crime, to a politely bored bar.

III

BILLBOARDS

> *It was some 180 metres from the site of*
> *this Motor Inn on the 24th October 1889*
> *that Sir Henry Parkes whilst Colonial Secretary*
> *and Past Member for Tenterfield*
> *made his famous and historic federation speech*
> *resulting in the formation of the Commonwealth of Australia.*
>
> *The Sydney Mail of the time*
> *quoted Sir Henry Parkes as*
> *Australia's most far sighted statesman.*
>
> *This Motor Inn is therefore named*
> *The Henry Parkes*

In Honour of this great statesman
A man to whom all Australians
should be proudly thankful
For the birth of a nation
In its own right.
A COLONY FOR A NATION AND A NATION FOR A COLONY.

(restaurant plaque, Henry Parkes Motor Inn)

∎

There was a legend still circulating in town when I was a child that the Tenterfield Oration was a myth. The Clerk of Petty Sessions, a man then old enough to have witnessed the event as a boy, would swear that Henry Parkes had merely ridden down the main street of Tenterfield, hopped off his horse, relieved himself around the back of the pub, then headed straight out for Sydney.

When locals laughed at the efforts of booster families to mark their patch as a Place of far-reaching significance, they made a joke with antecedents. In 1882 Parkes, returning from an exhausting voyage to America, Britain, and Europe to face turmoil over land reforms, lost the poll in East Sydney. The candidate for Tenterfield, a Mr Edward Reeves Whereat, JP, immediately stood aside and offered Parkes his seat. Elected unopposed, Parkes was baptized by his opponents 'The Member for *Whereat*'.

But the joke wasn't really on the Tenterfield boosters. Making an equation between progress for the town and rhetorical contiguity to a prominent figure, the *Tenterfield Star* celebrated Parkes's election by noting that it would assure its future as a transit-town: 'With regard to the Clarence and New England Railway, the return of Henry Parkes must necessarily make him a firm adherent to the Tenterfield route'.[33]

For far-flung communities dependent on transport for economic survival and growth, to be traversed and attract traversals was obviously a means to, and not an end of, the process of settling 'place'. The railway here didn't blur the landscape but made it visible, legible, and liveable to whites – cutting 'culture' into the bush. This dependence, though, is one reason why country towns never really acquired organic 'roots' or sentimental 'main street' connotations in Australian popular culture. The pomposities of civic pride remain defensive against the more powerful mythic pull of the routes for comings and goings.

Whether or not Parkes's 'adherence' to the route contributed to Tenterfield's success in becoming a transit-town, his name was firmly established as a patron saint of *passage*. In the circular production of 'prominence' that organized regional politics long before the arrival of media and regimes of simulation, the Tenterfield landowners, dignitaries, and small business families dined out on his story for decades. Modern tourism finds in their storytelling its basic semiotic strategy.

∎

In *The Practice of Everyday Life*, Michel de Certeau makes an interesting distinction between 'place' and 'space'. A *place* delimits a field; it is ruled by the law of the 'proper', by an orderly contiguity of elements in the location it defines, and as an instantaneous configuration of positions it implies an 'indication of stability'.[34]

A *space* is not the substance of a place but the product of its transformation. It exists only in relation to vectors of direction, velocities, and time variables. Space 'occurs'; composed of intersections of mobile elements, it is *actuated* by the ensemble of movements deployed within it. With none of the univocity or stability of the 'proper', it is produced by the operations that make it function in 'a polyvalent unity of conflictual programs or contractual proximities'.

'In short,' says de Certeau, 'space is a *practised place*.' The street defined by urban planning is transformed into a space by walkers; and, in the same way, an act of reading is a space produced by a practice of a written text (a 'place constituted by a system of signs').

One useful consequence of this definition is that no distinction can be made between authentic and 'inauthentic' places. At the same time, it avoids any move to predetermine the kind – and the tempo – of spatial (reading, walking) practices deemed 'appropriate' to particular places. A written text on a motel wall or restaurant plaque may be spatially practised in ways, in directions, and at velocities as various as any street, or literary text. By definition, no one spatial practice can correspond to a 'proper' use of place, and there are no exemplary users.

Nor is there a simple disjunction between the place and its use as space. For de Certeau, stories act as a means of transportation (*metaphorai*) in the shuttling that 'constantly transforms places into spaces or spaces into places'.

There are two sorts of determinations in stories. One works to found the law of place by the '*being-there* of something dead' – a pebble, a cadaver (or perhaps the record of a speech). The other works to specify spaces by the *actions* of historical subjects – stones, trees, human beings (or a political rogue in a hurry). There are passages back and forth between them – for example, in a story of the putting to death (or putting into a landscape) of heroes who have transgressed the law of the place, and make restoration with their tombs (or their epitaphs on motels).

That is, both determinations can be at work in any one legend or story. So the memorializing of events occurring at a site cannot simply be divided into, say, bad petty-bourgeois fabrication (myths of place, sacralization) and good popular contestation (semiotics of displacement, debunking). As an activity, memorializing is itself a complex spatial-story practice. Struggles (conflictual programmes) occur in the shuttling between stories, and between competing determinations *in* stories. Thus the rival versions of the Tenterfield Oration ('Call to the Nation' versus 'Call of Nature') both commemorate a local event and invest a site with meaning, but the second *enlivens* the first – as well as marking its enshrinement of a something-dead as a socially placed aspiration (rather than a 'national' event).

This distinction can be useful in dismantling those lingering equations between the place and the *domus*, displacement and the voyage, which in recent years have made the projects of feminist history so fraught, despite the rhetoric of the local, with general-theoretical anxiety[35] – particularly since de Certeau's concept of story operates at the level of minute phrases and tiny events as well as larger narrative structures. His insistence that 'every story is a travel story – a spatial practice' (p. 115) refers to sentences, footsteps, or scraps of TV news rather than vast developmental schemas for ordering human life.

Thus he differentiates between 'tours' and 'maps', not in terms of teleological narrative drives in the one case and fixations of the Present in the other, but as competing modalities in a process of narrative description. In 'oral descriptions of places, narrations concerning the home, stories about the streets',[36] for example, indicators of the 'map' type ('There is a historic site 180 metres down the road') present tableaux (*seeing* as 'the knowledge of an order of places'), while those of the 'tour' type ('You go down to the School of Arts') organize movements (*going* as 'spatializing actions'). In narration, one form may be dominant but punctuated by the other: tours postulate maps, while maps condition and presuppose tours. It is their combination in a narrative chain of spatializing operations that defines for de Certeau the structure of the travel story: 'stories of journeys and actions are marked out by the "citation" of the places that result from them or authorize them' (p. 120).

The travel story, therefore, does not consist of process contained and directed by origin and destination, nor does it oscillate between 'perspectives' on reality. It is itself a movement organized (like any spatial story) between both prospective and retrospective mappings of place *and* the practices that transform them.

■

Various foundation stories wander around the Henry Parkes (on brochures, cards, and a menu in all the rooms) as well as up and down the streets. The front-wall legend, with its war-memorial layout and assertive historical statement, transmutes on a restaurant plaque into the visual form of a poem.

In this text, events are elegiacally distanced by a *tournure* of romance. It begins from place, not time ('It was some 180 metres . . .' versus 'On the 24th October . . .'); and an archaizing syntax ('history-effect') combines with a proprietorial enunciative trace in a discourse of obligation ('all Australians should be proudly thankful'). This produces an aura of special importance, like saying grace before the meal. But it also makes the restaurant plaque a declaration of personal commitment rather than a simple touristic seduction.[37]

The plaque has another touch, however, which marks it off from the other stories and yet defines the type of movement that regulates them all.

It ends with a kind of slogan: 'A COLONY FOR A NATION AND A NATION FOR A COLONY.' It's a resonant, and memorable, phrase. But, when you stop to think, it doesn't make sense – or, rather, it maps an imaginary place. It works for a world in which New South Wales alone became 'Australia', or in which the whole of the Australian continent was occupied by one vast colony. Either way, the whole process of federating six distinct and mutually suspicious colonies into one nation would have been (like the Tenterfield Oration) quite unnecessary.

It could be called a misquotation. The original slogan, attributed to Edmund Barton (later to be first Prime Minister), was 'For the first time in history, we have *a nation for a continent and a continent for a nation.*' But this production of congruence between natural and political places occurred in a public speech. It begins its course of citation and recitation in Australian historiography not as a text certified by its author but as a reported 'memorable impromptu' made at a meeting. In his memoirs, Robert Randolph Garran claimed to have been its first inscriber: it 'would have been unrecorded if I had not happened to write it down'.[38]

What matters in this story is not a myth of the primacy of the spoken word but the movement (in this case, of hearsay) that runs between citings of the text – and that movement in one place of its migration, a plaque on a dining-room wall, transforms it from place-founding slogan to the 'score' of a lilting rhythm: a trill, a whistle, a jingle, a musical spatial story.

■

If you follow the story down the street and go on a tour of the town, several maps of the present and stories of the past begin to intersect. There's discord about it, not just a codified diversity-and-difference.

The School of Arts enshrines the site of Parkes's speech. It's disconcerting to enter with any sense of anticipation, for the inside turns out to be an everyday lending library. As Dean MacCannell points out, the most difficult sights to sacralize are places where something once happened (battles, speech events) but where there's nothing left to see. All that's left here is a lovely but still walked-on original wooden floor.

Down one end, however, there is a roped-off tiny museum of Henry Parkes memorabilia. Apart from a 1915 bust, and a portrait of Parkes in his favourite pose as a late Victorian Moses, most of the objects (wheelbarrow, dog collar, watch) seem to have been collected on the basis of their having been *touched* by Parkes or by persons in his vicinity. They are those objects most confusing and emotionally opaque to a media sensibility – genuine relics. But even this image of sanctum is jarred by pieces which seem to have nothing personal to do with Parkes: a modern book on *Georgian Architecture*, local histories of distant places, bits of twentieth-century pottery with a nationalistic theme. It's a museum dedicated not to the remains of a person but to an old school of history – an inventory of unrelated, age-encrusted, national *faits divers*.

A few blocks away, a rival foundation-place offers something more familiar. It's a showbiz monument – an old shop restored as the home of the 'Tenterfield Saddler'. Built in the 1860s, it was created a few years ago from a song by an American-based entertainer, Peter Allen (commemorating a family connection). It's an impeccable third-order simulacrum: even though the building is now 'in its original condition', it reproduces an image of a reality with no previous claim to existence. People treat it respectfully as a forebear of Tenterfield's modernity.

The Centenary Cottage museum tries for something completely different. It has long been in transition between an old house crammed with junk and a 'restored pioneer home'. An incipient programme is readable: the highway-oriented, universalizing pedagogy of simulation hovers as a possibility. But, even in the rooms already most organized towards this ideal, the period-effect is overwhelmed by local genealogies. In a clear case of what MacCannell calls 'obliteration by the markers', each item is cluttered by the history of its donation: a bed is presented by A, handmade by B from a silky oak cut on property C located at D in 1881, and restored by Mr and Mrs E. This museum is unreadable to outsiders. It refuses to efface the gestures of labour, ownership, and gift in the manner essential to catching transient interests – not because it has a deep-rooted sense of 'reality', but because it has no idea of its own obscurity. This is a *dynastic* museum – a 'who's who here' display – and despite its touristic ambitions it primarily lectures the town.

Nothing much here means anything to me. But in the more disorganized parts of the Cottage two objects immediately provoke what is usually called 'nostalgia'.

One is in the yard, past an old weighing machine stranded in the grass and some singed-looking ferns by a drain. It's an old laundry copper, 'historic', but intimately stifling: hot, heavy, stubborn loads of washing to be stirred, stick circling round boiling water, in a misery of blazing heat every endless Saturday morning.

The other is in the chaos of junk inside. Next to a 1921 income-tax receipt are the 'Last Reservation Tickets for the Lyric Theatre'. My own first cinema memory rushes up from the 1950s. But it has nothing to do with hurtling through space, zooming through time, or an aesthetics of disappearance.

It's about *placement*, a memory of anxiety in the theatre about where to sit, just the same as in the schoolroom. A tension map of proximities to avoid: town Aborigines (all right, sort of); white West End louts (worse); and worst, in a row tacitly off-limits to everyone else, the Aboriginal and white-trash families from just out of town on The Common.

■

If within a few blocks it's possible to tour an archaic mode of pedagogy, a parochial display of current class and caste distinctions, and a piece of postmodern aesthetics, then it is partly because tourism here is as yet barely organized. Apart from National Parks and National Trust (historic buildings) activity, tourism operates as a local response to economic distress.[39] It's also relatively innocuous – though there's something devastating about the blatancy of a leaflet available around town called *The Bluff Rock Massacre*. 'We punished them severely, and proved our superiority to them', proudly cites the local historian, blending geological details of the rock with the tale of a 'tribe' being thrown from the top. A more sophisticated tourist operation would obliterate that immediately.

But, if their haphazard efforts make country towns eccentric to the global tourist economy, they also suggest a general difficulty in constructing guides to the Present, or theories of the tourist homing instinct. It isn't just that they are obdurately *there*, waiting in ambush like the suburbs on the edge of the metropolis, with their own declarations of reality. It's rather that even in the smallest places, where the production of space involves a limited number of 'conflictual programs and contractual proximities', in de Certeau's phrase, the operative *simultaneity* of programmes and proximities makes the effort to take any one as exemplary (either of the Now, or of a 'domestication' of history in myth) only one of the more aggressively territorial programmes competing to found its place.

Thousands of miles away, Jean Baudrillard writes in *Amérique*: 'Why go off to decentralize myself in France with the ethnic and the local, among the scraps and remains of centrality?' He wants to become ex-centred in the centre of the world. Fair enough. But when he gets there he finds, like a postmodern mystic, the universe in a Burgerking crumb – or a Studebaker, or an empty motel. His America is a 'gigantic hologram ... all the information contained in each of its elements'.[40] I do know what he means. Even in an Australian country town – a vestige of failed decentralization rather than a residue of centrality – I can see something of All Australia in the Saddlery, or the becoming-Burgerking of the old Greek café down the road.

But the point about holograms (like simulacra) is that they volatilize, rather than re-place, other models of signifying practice (spatial stories). In fact, a hologram is one of the visual events least able to admit of relations in contiguity: it is defined (in Baudrillard's description) by an absolute self-containment. It really doesn't recognize the logic of the *next* – hologram here, cinema next door, painting over there – which activates spaces in contemporary culture and makes philosophies of grounding so difficult to sustain. It is a traffic in negotiable proximities (temporal as well as spatial) between conflicting practices that follows from the decentring of a Renaissance 'perspective' on life – and not the restoration of hierarchy by a controlling reference-point that marginalizes the 'rest'.

A motel is a good place in which to consider the question of traffic, precisely because it is consecrated to proximity and circulation. It is neither the car nor the highway nor the house nor the voyage nor the home, but a space of movements between all of them. It punctuates travelling with resting and being-there with action. It represents neither 'arrival' nor 'departure', but operates passages from one to the other in the *metaphorai* of the pause. Motel-time is a syncopation of different speeds in varied degrees of duration.

But it is not an exemplary site – precisely because it only exists transitionally, in any usage, between other possibilities. It provides an operational link not only between practices but between institutions. In countless fictional motels, gangsters, lovers, psychopaths, drifters, and defaulters come to motels to be killed, seized, abandoned, or imprisoned as well as to hide, to escape, to recover – in transit between many kinds of prison, and many attempts at release. So, despite its resonance for highway romance, the motel may always, in the end, affirm the being-there of the place and the modalities of the map – but it creates the possibility of the tour.

■

In recent articles Lawrence Grossberg has used the model of the roadside billboard to pose problems about interpreting events in popular culture and the politics of everyday life.

Billboards, for Grossberg, are 'markers' (neither authentic nor inauthentic) that are there to be driven by. They don't tell us where we are going, but yet they mark, and comprise, boundaries; they are the outside, inside, and limits of the town that they announce and that we are passing through. They advertise, yet we drive past without paying attention to what they say because we already know, or because it doesn't matter. Yet they do tell us what road we are on, and they reaffirm that we are actually moving. They are not there to be interpreted or 'read'; yet they are a space in which many different discourses appear (so they are sites of struggle). But any *individual* billboard is in-different. It is 'neither built upon a radical sense of textual difference, nor does it erase all difference.'[41]

So Grossberg suggests that interpreting the politics and effects of popular culture is less like reading a book than like driving by billboards – not because the street is the only reality, but because billboards belong simultaneously to the orders of local detail and national structure, and connect to places off the road (factories, gaols, houses). Billboards are also like the bric-à-brac in Centenary Cottage – apparently meaningless 'signposts' which, for all the irrelevance and seeming uselessness of their specific inscriptions, become sites of investment and empowerment (not necessarily benevolent). For Grossberg, such signposts make it possible to continue struggling to *make* a difference, by devising 'mattering maps'.

So if billboards (unlike the motel) are dominated by the operationality of space and the modality of the tour (by 'going' rather than 'seeing') they enable in turn the making of maps, the citing and seeing of places.

This image is all the more useful if we remember that, as well as driving by billboards anywhere, people sometimes stop near particular billboards somewhere – live near them, photograph them, picnic and read books beside them, deface them, or even (near Tenterfield) shoot at them.

For most of the 1980s, the limits of Tenterfield were marked on the three main roads by 'National (The Big Entertainer)' billboards. They ringed the town with images of Peter Allen at the piano, declaring that he 'Still Called Australia Home', and that Tenterfield was the Home of the Tenterfield Saddler. These routine, concentric productions of Place from the figure of Allen (Saddler/Tenterfield/Australia) were in perfect conformity with the older myth of Henry Parkes (Motel/Tenterfield/Australia). In 1987 they were replaced by billboards advertising a nearby natural wonder, Bald Rock (Australia's Largest Granite Rock) – each separately handpainted in the perfect image of its postcard by two women artists from Tenterfield. For a while, at least, these three serialized 'individual' billboards will figure on local mattering maps – not as in-different signposts enabling the making of difference, but as signs (for those to whom it matters) of a difference *made*. That they may revert, in time, to in-difference makes no difference to the spatial story.

■

Once out at the billboards, the tourist could go home to the Henry Parkes Motel, home to her mother's place nearby, or head home on the road to Sydney. Each ending might define a different kind of domesticity: formalist (return to first principles), feminist (return to a place of origin), or postmodernist (Blase admits the transience of her interest in small towns, and reclaims her intellectual mobility). All of these resolutions might be perfectly realistic.

In any case, I can drive away still thinking about Henry Parkes, of whom I've had very little to say. My interest has been in the disjunctions between the rhetorics of movement, displacement, and rapidity in debates about popular culture, and the feminist insistence on recognizing place in critiques of everyday life. But, if so, it is because there is a political stake in the awkward relations between them.

The problem for feminism might be summed up by Prato and Trivero's claim in 'The spectacle of travel' that transport ceased to be a metaphor of Progress when *mobility* came to characterize everyday life more than the image of 'home and family'. Transport became, instead, 'the primary activity of existence'.[42] Feminism has no need whatsoever to claim home-and-family as its special preserve, but it does imply a certain discretion about proclaiming its present marginalization.

It's possible to argue, for example, that in Australia (and in many places) the mobility/*domus* distinction is at best historically doubtful. It is mobility as a *means* of endlessly making prospects (or 'progress') for home-and-family that becomes, for many people, the primary activity of existence. And colonization may be precisely a mode of movement (as occupation) that transgresses limits and borders. In and after colonialism, the voyage/*domus* distinction loses its oppositional structure – and thus its value for announcing the displacement of one by the other in the 'course' of Human History.

Yet the sort of claim being made by Prato and Trivero does not seek its grounding in historical 'truth' – even the truth of approximation – and thus makes feminist criticism more difficult. It is meant, perhaps, to be a billboard, a marker in a certain landscape. It marks a recognizable trajectory along which it becomes possible not only for some to think their lives as a trip on a road to nowhere (etc.), but for others to think home-and-family as a comfortable, 'empowering' vehicle.

So, rather than retreating to the invidious position of trying to contradict a billboard, feminist criticism might make its own. I have two in mind – two textual places that might be transformed by a shuttle between them producing a spatial story.

As individual billboards, they don't tell me anything in particular – not how to read the history of the family, tourism, or Australian politics, and certainly not how to read the relations between political change and the persistent vagrancy of clichés. But together they mark out space for considering convergence and overlap, rather than divergence and distinction, between the rhetoric of mobility and the politics of placement, the mapping of the voyage and the 'metaphorics of *home*'.

One is a quotation from Henry Parkes – self-made man, traveller, family man, Premier, modernizer, philosopher, and Father of Federation – who spoke of the political reforms of the 1860s in these terms:

> *Our business being to colonize the country, there was only one way to do it – by spreading over it all the associations and connections of family life.*[43]

The other is a media anecdote from the *Sydney Morning Herald* last year, entitled 'Great moments in philosophy'.[44] Paul Keating – self-made man, family man, Federal Treasurer, modernizer, philosopher, Deregulationist – refuted accusations that he was using his travelling allowance to purchase antique clocks. Asked why he claimed travel refunds when he lived in Canberra with his home-and-family, he replied on the steps of Parliament House:

> *We are wayfarers on one long road. Mere wayfarers.*

Sydney, 1987

Notes

Thanks to Joyce Morris, Colin Hood, and Anne Zahalka.

1 Some material in this essay is from a forthcoming book about myths of progress in Australia, which will include a more developed study of the figure of Parkes.

 Henry Parkes (1815–96) came with his wife to Australia from Birmingham as an assisted immigrant in 1838–9. He was a penniless artisan, and, despite several efforts at business in Australia, he spent much of his life on the verge and over the edge of bankruptcy. He was a member of the Birmingham Mechanics' Institute, and was influenced by the early phases of Chartism. As his biographer A. W. Martin points out (*Henry Parkes* (Melbourne: Melbourne University Press, 1980)), the timing of his emigration left him, 'for good, a Birmingham man of 1832 rather than of 1839: a radical, but dedicated to middle and working class co-operation as the key to reform and progress' (p. 17).

 During a political career which lasted from 1848 till his death, he was five times Premier of New South Wales – presiding over the implementation of most of the ideals he had arrived with, as well as of a pro-white, pro-Anglican (anti-coloured, anti-Catholic) vision of Australia's destiny. He ended in the 1890s as an arch-conservative, utterly baffled by the Labor Party.

 He married three times, and fathered the last of seventeen children at the age of 77.

Needless to say, his 1889 speech did not cause Australian Federation. His reasons for making it seem to have been at least partly opportunistic, and the speech itself had at best a symbolic effect in galvanizing public interest in the matter, particularly in NSW.

2 Iain Chambers, *Popular Culture: The Metropolitan Experience* (London and New York: Methuen, 1986), p. 12.

3 Dean MacCannell, *The Tourist: A New Theory of the Leisure Class* (New York: Schocken, 1976).

4 Georges Van den Abbeele, 'Sightseers: the tourist as theorist', *Diacritics*, 10 (December 1980), p. 13.

5 Robert Venturi, Denise Scott Brown, and Steven Izenour, *Learning from Las Vegas: The Forgotten Symbolism of Architectural Form* (Cambridge, Mass.: MIT Press, 1977), pp. 34–5.

6 Daniel Boorstin, *The Image: A Guide to Pseudo-Events in America* (New York: Harper & Row, 1961). See also the critique of Boorstin in MacCannell, op. cit., pp. 102–7.

7 'Places are odd and call for interpretation. . . . Pseudo-places entice by their familiarity and call for instant recognition': Paul Fussell, *Abroad: British Literary Traveling Between the Wars* (New York and Oxford: Oxford University Press, 1980), p. 43.

8 Jean Baudrillard, 'The precession of simulacra', in *Simulations* (New York: Semiotext(e), 1983); also in *Art & Text*, 11 (Spring 1983), pp. 3–47. Baudrillard makes explicit reference to Boorstin in *La Société de consommation* (Paris: Gallimard, 1970).

9 Paolo Prato and Gianluca Trivero, 'The spectacle of travel', *The Australian Journal of Cultural Studies*, 3, 2 (December 1985), p. 27.

10 Paul Virilio, 'Véhiculaire', in *Cause commune, nomades et vagabonds* (Paris: UGE 10/18, 1975), p. 52; my translation.

11 Richard Sieburth, 'Sentimental travelling: on the road (and off the wall) with Laurence Sterne', *Scripsi*, 4, 3 (1987), p. 203.

12 In both Paul Virilio's *Esthétique de la disparition* (Paris: Balland, 1980) and Jean Baudrillard's *Amérique* (Paris: Grasset, 1986), the traditional connection between the perceptual shifts brought about by cinema and rapid transport is developed in terms of *disappearance*. For Virilio – concerned with movement in the history of militarization rather than tourism – the invention of the camera is also associated with the chrono-photographic rifle and the Gatling gun: *Pure War* (New York: Semiotext(e), 1983), pp. 82–3.

13 Paul Virilio, *Vitesse et politique* (Paris, Galilée, 1977), pp. 18–19. Virilio's term is actually *implantation*. He argues that the strategic implantation of the fixed domicile is more important to the historical formation of bourgeois power than commerce or industrialism.

14 Venturi, Scott Brown, and Izenour, op. cit., pp. 34–5.

15 See Anthony Giddens, *The Constitution of Society* (Cambridge and Oxford: Polity Press, 1984), pp. 122–6. See also MacCannell, op. cit., pp. 91–102.

16 See C. M. H. Clark, *A History of Australia*, vol. 5: *The People Make Laws 1888–1915* (Melbourne: Melbourne University Press, 1981); A. W. Martin, *Henry Parkes: A Biography* (Melbourne: Melbourne University Press, 1980); and, on country towns and myths of progress, Donald Horne, *Money Made Us* (Harmondsworth: Penguin, 1976).

17 John Robertson and Charles Cowper, factional leaders in the NSW parliament. Colonial politics was organized not by a party system but around vying

personalities. Henry Parkes, *Studies in Rhyme* (Sydney: J. Ferguson, 1870).

18 Van den Abbeele, op. cit., p. 9. Subsequent page references to this appear in the text in parentheses.

19 MacCannell, op. cit., p. 3. Subsequent page references to this appear in the text in parentheses.

20 This is one of the ways in which a hierarchical distinction between 'travelling' and 'tourism' is frequently maintained. In Jean Baudrillard's *Amérique* (Paris: Grasset, 1986), 'Nothing is more alien to pure travelling than tourism or leisure' (p. 24). For Baudrillard, the tourist, not the traveller, is an archaic figure, still searching for meaning, reason, and reality.

21 Sam Shepard, *Motel Chronicles* (San Francisco: City Lights Books, 1982), p. 102.

22 Neither writer pays much attention to the 'work' of the leisure industry, or considers the problem of domestic labour in relation to either industrial production or 'post-industrial' production. Doing so might have made the industrial/post-industrial line more difficult to draw. Instead, domestic labour is simply subsumed, by implication, in the shift from 'work' to 'leisure'.

23 An example of the political complexity of tourism was provided after the military coup in Fiji in May 1987, when efforts at economic protest on behalf of the former government were undermined by the immediate introduction of cut-price air-fares from Australia. It is interesting to wonder to what extent touristic imperviousness to a coup in a nearby country can count as a danger to *Australian* 'integrity'.

24 Biddy Martin and Chandra Talpade Mohanty, 'Feminist politics: what's home got to do with it?', in Teresa de Lauretis (ed.), *Feminist Studies/Critical Studies* (Bloomington: Indiana University Press, 1986), pp. 193–4.

25 Menie Parkes, *Poems, Printed for Private Circulation* (Sydney, 1867). See A. W. Martin (ed.), *Letters from Menie: Sir Henry Parkes and his Daughter* (Melbourne: Melbourne University Press, 1983).

26 Iain Chambers, 'Maps for the metropolis: a possible guide to the present', *Cultural Studies*, 1, 1 (January 1987), pp. 1–21. Page references to this appear in the text in parentheses.

27 Chambers, *Popular Culture*, p. 13.

28 Angus Fletcher, *Allegory: The Theory of a Symbolic Mode* (Ithaca and London: Cornell University Press, 1964), p. 35. Subsequent page references to this appear in the text in parentheses.

29 Cited in Donna Haraway, 'A manifesto for cyborgs: science, technology and socialist feminism in the 1980s', *Socialist Review*, 80 (1985); reprinted in *Australian Feminist Studies*, 4 (Autumn 1987).

30 Regretful notation of the predominantly 'masculine' orientation of popular culture seems to be Iain Chambers's main response to the kind of criticism made some years ago by Angela McRobbie, in 'Settling accounts with subcultures' (*Screen Education*, 34 (Spring 1980), pp. 37–49). The problem, however, may not be a matter of the objective masculinity of the streets and whether women are or are not getting out there too, so much as it is a problem with the *model* of 'popular culture' being derived (or imposed) from a limited range of experience. For women at windows, see Dick Hebdige, 'The impossible object: towards a sociology of the sublime', *New Formations*, 1 (Spring 1987), pp. 47–76.

31 Haraway, op. cit.

32 Frank Moorhouse, *Room Service: Comic Writings of Frank Moorhouse* (Harmondsworth: Penguin, 1985), p. 52.

33 *Tenterfield Star*, 6 December 1882; cited in Norman Crawford, *Tenterfield* (Tenterfield District Historical Society, 1949).

34 Michel de Certeau, *The Practice of Everyday Life*, trans. Steven F. Rendall (Berkeley and London: University of California Press, 1984), pp. 117 ff. Subsequent page references to this appear in the text in parentheses.

35 See Martin and Talpade Mohanty, op. cit.

36 De Certeau, op. cit., pp. 118–20. De Certeau borrows the tour/map distinction from Linde and Labov's study of apartment descriptions by New York residents: 'spatial networks as a rite for the study of language and thought', *Language*, 51 (1975), pp. 924–39..

37 The motel was in fact built by a couple whose family had known Henry Parkes in his heyday, but well before he was knighted. So the motel is named simply the Henry Parkes, in order to represent appropriately the nature of the family connection.

38 R. R. Garran, *Prosper the Commonwealth* (Sydney: Angus & Robertson, 1958), p. 101.

39 Like many country towns, Tenterfield – faced with decline in agriculture, sensitivity in the timber industry, and closure of the local meatworks – talked in the 1970s about the possibility of its own extinction. Natural and historical 'resources' then began to be mapped for a semiotics of attraction. If the highway brings fewer commercial transports in search of wood and meat, it now brings more urban transients in search of trees, animals, the homes of pioneers. The town adjusted quite successfully, although many residents depend on social security to survive.

40 Baudrillard, *Amérique*, pp. 56, 59.

41 Lawrence Grossberg, 'The in-difference of television', *Screen*, 28 (Spring 1987), pp. 28–45. See also his 'Putting the pop back into postmodernism', in Andrew Ross (ed.), *Universal Abandon?* (Minneapolis: University of Minnesota Press, forthcoming). Grossberg uses billboards as a way of discussing the gap between 'ideological' and 'affective' maps.

42 Prato and Trivero, op. cit., p. 40.

43 New South Wales Legislative Assembly, 14 August 1866; cited in Stephen Murray-Smith (ed.), *The Dictionary of Australian Quotations* (Melbourne: Heinemann, 1984), p. 211.

44 'Stay in touch', *Sydney Morning Herald*, 30 June 1987.

AT HENRY PARKES MOTEL 47

JENNY WOLMARK

ALTERNATIVE FUTURES?
SCIENCE FICTION AND
FEMINISM

Science fiction has been a notoriously male-dominated area of popular fiction for so long that the idea of feminist science fiction seems to be almost a contradiction in terms. In many ways feminist science fiction is at odds with the whole history and development of SF as a genre which, by virtually excluding women, has imposed very real limitations on their actual and potential contribution. So it seems to me that the relatively recent phenomenon of a distinctly feminist SF, as opposed to SF written by those writers who also happen to be women, represents an important cultural intervention on the part of feminists, and a significant expression of the impact of feminism on popular fiction. As such, it is a necessary part of the wider process of re-evaluating popular fiction as a whole and, in particular, popular fiction written by and for women.

The development of SF as popular fiction has in general been dominated by writers and readers with a knowledge of science and engineering and a commitment to the idea that technology is the motor of social change and progress. The attachment of SF readers and writers to the notion that science is an innately progressive and civilizing force resulted in the production of a great many stories involving fairly crude extrapolations of contemporary ideas and attitudes from the present to the future. This kind of SF, often repetitive and formulaic, reproduced the most conservative assumptions about social and sexual relations and imposed severe limitations on the nature of the popular readership that SF could expect. Not only was the readership mostly male but it was also very small. Under these conditions, the contribution that women could make was minimal, so much so that women who did wish to have SF stories published often had to do so under a male pseudonym – an interesting echo of the position that many nineteenth-century women novelists found themselves in. André Norton, for example, changed her name from Alice to encourage ambiguity about her gender and, more recently, James Tiptree, Jr, was revealed to be Alice Sheldon.

That situation has undergone some change since the 1960s, particularly with the advent of the so-called New Wave SF writers, who introduced into

SF different social and political concerns and alternative fictional strategies and techniques which appealed to a much wider and noticeably more heterogeneous audience. It is ironic that in recent years some SF writers and critics have used the massive popularity that SF currently enjoys to argue that SF should no longer be considered as popular fiction at all but should be incorporated instead into mainstream fiction, on the basis that the thematic and stylistic concerns of SF bear an undeniable similarity to those of 'serious' literature. While this argument appears to signal some kind of recognition of changes in the genre and the readership of SF, in reality it constitutes a straightforward reproduction of existing critical hierarchies and polarities between serious and popular fiction. The focus on the literary credentials of SF reveals a dependence on a definition of 'Literature' that, within the dominant ideology, constructs it as the idealized and privileged repository of literary value; this effectively obscures both the historical specificity of literary production and the ideological discourses that it contains. No account is taken of the relationship between changes in the genre itself and those transformations that are taking place elsewhere in both social relations and cultural practices. In the case of SF, the comfortable complacency this produces enables critics to ignore the changes to the genre that have been brought about because of the specific involvement of women in both the production and the consumption of SF. The result of this is the continued marginalization of women and their 'absence' as gendered subjects from the texts.

It is this marginalization in cultural practice that feminism challenges, not least by encouraging a general political interest in women writers and the social and historical conditions of their literary production and consumption. By means of what has been called a 'gender-inflected reading strategy',[1] feminists have demonstrated that texts can be read for their alternative and potential meanings rather than in terms of a single dominant meaning. This strategy has been used extensively by feminist literary critics to provoke a general reconsideration of many major literary texts by revealing the way in which those texts can be seen to articulate areas of women's experience under patriarchy. However, the implications of a feminist mode of reading extend beyond the boundaries of literary criticism. It is particularly important where popular fiction is concerned, and yet this is an area that has been largely ignored by feminist literary critics, partly because it is judged to be an inferior kind of literature but also because it is assumed that popular fiction unproblematically reproduces dominant patriarchal attitudes to women.

This kind of judgement has been most marked in the case of the most female-oriented kind of popular fiction, the romance, and the critical distinction made between a 'female gothic' literary tradition and its less serious popular variant, romance fiction, has, until recently, encountered very little opposition. Although male-oriented popular genres like the thriller or the western have received some critical analysis, in comparison the major genre for women, the romance, is too often dismissed as being escapist and trivial. Certainly the way in which romance fiction is marketed has something to do with this attitude. The novels are often sold under the brand name of the publisher and within the general category of 'romance', rather than as individual titles – which inevitably suggests the formulaic quality of the narratives. However, it is not the repetitious nature of the stories in themselves that needs emphasizing but the contradictory relationship of the narratives to the real social and material conditions of their own existence and that of their readers. A feminist mode of reading that is not bound by the traditional categories of literary criticism can offer this kind of perspective. Recent studies of romance fiction[2] provide very interesting examples of how this can work by looking at the way in which the fiction consistently puts forward the imaginary solutions of love and marriage to 'solve' the real problem of the social, cultural, and economic repression of women. These narratives idealize self-sacrificing domesticity as the most desirable option open to women and indicate that a woman's happiness lies in the achievement of this. But the overt idealization of these imaginary solutions generates incoherences and tensions within the stories which draw attention to what the texts themselves repress: that the real contradiction in many women's lives is that such domesticity, far from being desirable, is often the *only* option open to women if they are to achieve some measure of economic security. The internal contradictions in the stories are the result of attempts within the fiction to give coherence to an ideological construction of gender which is itself at odds with the historical and material reality of women in patriarchal society.

There are other aspects of the contradictory nature of romance fiction which may partly account for the real pleasure that readers derive from these novels. The pursuit of personal happiness, while it is often put forward in a problematic way in the novels because it excludes everything else, has a more positive side to it, in that the desire for a fulfilling and loving relationship is affirmed as being a worthy ideal. Because they imaginatively remove all obstacles between desire and its fulfilment, the narratives cannot help but contain utopian possibilities. Equally important is the fact that the central characters in romance narratives are women, and the focus of the narratives is on their emotions and ambitions rather than on those of the male characters. However ultimately conservative and contradictory the roles for women are in romance fiction, this female-centred focus is an important aspect of their appeal for women.

From the example of romance fiction, it should be clear that a feminist mode of reading does not mean reading popular fiction as an inferior version of Literature, nor does it mean reading popular fiction as an unmediated expression of the dominant ideology. Instead, it suggests that what is required is a historically specific way of reading and understanding popular fiction which can provide the means to explore the social and ideological relations of both texts and readers.

The perspective that such a reading strategy can provide is very useful when applied to science fiction. As was previously suggested, SF is not usually thought of as women's fiction, but recent changes in the production of SF and its audience indicate that this is perhaps no longer the case.

Increasing numbers of women now read and write science fiction, and, more significantly, a specifically feminist intervention into SF has been made on the part of some of those writers. A number of women's publishing presses have been set up from the 1970s onwards in America and Britain, and these have largely made this intervention possible. The Women's Press, for example, has started to publish a science-fiction list which includes reprints of feminist SF mostly unavailable previously in Britain. The new marketing strategies and outlets introduced by the women's presses have undoubtedly had an impact on the network of institutional relationships that exist between publishers, writers, and readers, and this has had the general effect of broadening the definition of what constitutes 'women's fiction'. Feminist SF should be seen as part of the popularizing of SF across a wider and more heterogeneous audience which has been going on since the 1960s, and is therefore in a very interesting position: it has the potential to address both a specifically female audience and a far wider popular audience. It exists at a kind of intersection between feminist and popular readings of narratives. While there are inevitable contradictions in such a position, it does seem to suggest that feminism and popular fiction are not as wholly incompatible as has previously been proposed.

In her book on the subversive quality of fantasy, Rosemary Jackson emphasizes the importance of non-realist writing for feminists: 'No breakthrough of cultural structure seems possible until linear narrative (realism, illusionism, transparent representation) is broken or dissolved.'[3] According to this view, realism, as the dominant convention in popular narratives, would appear to impose an insurmountable barrier between feminists and the readers and writers of popular narratives. This unduly pessimistic conclusion does not consider the possibility that realism is not a fixed category but a convention that can be reworked to contain oppositional meanings. Realism is a rhetorical strategy which, while it does reproduce the values of the dominant patriarchal ideology, can also be used to call those values into question.

In order to develop this point, I want to look at the work of a group of women SF writers who write conventional SF narratives yet manage to challenge the kinds of assumptions on which such narratives are based. The writers I shall be discussing are C. J. Cherryh, James Tiptree, Jr, Suzy McKee Charnas, Sally Miller Gearhart, Vonda McIntyre, and Joanna Russ. The narrative structures and conventions that provide a lot of the pleasure for readers of science fiction are also used by these writers, but they are used in an attempt to shift the focus of that pleasure away from the conventional expectations about social and sexual relations that are built into such narratives and towards alternative and non-patriarchal assumptions. The SF novels of C. J. Cherryh, for example, are full of women characters who are space pilots, soldiers, battlefleet commanders, and so on. The roles themselves may be familiar in SF narratives, but the fact that women fill these roles is not. Because they are the kind of roles that are usually reserved for male characters in SF narratives, the reader's expectations of the narratives are disturbed. What is noticeable about C. J. Cherryh's stories is that there is no recourse to the standard narrative devices used to suggest that these are socially and sexually unacceptable roles for women. Isaac Asimov, for example, uses just such a device in *I, Robot*, where the robotics expert, Dr Susan Calvin, is described in terms which deliberately suggest that her intellectual ability is achieved at the expense of her femininity: 'She was a frosty girl, plain and colorless, who protected herself against a world she disliked by a mask-like expression and hypertrophy of intellect.'[4]

In Cherryh's stories, the narratives are actually structured around the idea that not only is it both rational and feasible that women should have such roles but that this necessitates a reconstruction of relations between the sexes. At a certain level, then, these narratives are quite capable of subverting the dominant ideology of gender. In *Merchanter's Luck* (1984) the two main characters, Sandor and Allison, are not developed by Cherryh in terms of the existing range of male and female stereotypes in SF, and in order to undermine narrative expectations of gender differences both are given similar roles as crew members of spaceships. Allison is not only efficient and effective in her job; she is also presented as being sexually and socially assertive and independent. Sandor is presented in an equally untypical way: although he is depicted as a 'loner', he is not given any of the usual attributes associated with this stereotypical male role. Instead, he is shown as being socially isolated, sexually vulnerable, unambitious, and not given to the outbursts of heroic violence that one might expect from such a character. The unconventional characterization has an unsettling effect because the narrative itself is an entirely conventional SF story concerning the foiling of an attempt by renegade troops to hijack a space station. The contrast between the unfamiliar characterization and the wholly familiar story-line works to disrupt prevailing assumptions which are based on those ideologically constructed definitions of gender which are an integral part of the genre.

This disruption can be seen even more clearly in Cherryh's *The Pride of Chanur* (1983).[5] Although the narrative is once again conventional enough, the central characters are highly unconventional. Not only are they all female but they are members of a non-human race who have claws, fur, beards, and manes. They are captain and crew of the ship *Chanur's Pride* because, in a nice touch of irony, the males of the species are too temperamentally unstable to go into space. The crew of each ship is made up of members of an extended family group, the female head of which becomes the ship's captain. The narrative centres on one such head, Pyanfar Chanur, and is told largely from her point of view. The reader is given an unexpected perspective from which to engage with the story, which concerns a stowaway who is found on the ship. Tully, the stowaway, is human, but because of the point of view established in the narrative he is seen as alien, not only because he is human but also because he is male. So the narrative positions the male as both alien *and* outsider, and as such he is rendered powerless. Contrary to the expectations generated by the otherwise conventional narrative, Tully does not assert himself to take on more heroic proportions. He remains a powerless alien, totally dependent on the care of others for his wellbeing. The perspective offered by the narrative is both disconcerting and disrupting for SF readers: the male character that readers would expect to identify with remains a shadowy figure, and the familiar SF convention of the alien is used to shift the focus of the narrative in such a way that the real subject of the narrative becomes a fascinating and playful examination of the way in which gender is socially and culturally determined.

The well-known short story by James Tiptree, Jr, 'Houston, Houston, do you read?' (1978), contains a similarly disconcerting perspective operating within a conventional narrative. The story concerns the three-man crew of an American spacecraft which, because of solar-flare activity, is accidentally thrust 300 years into the future and is rescued by a ship which has an all-female crew. Tiptree uses the central enigma of the unknown nature of this future earth ironically to reveal the way in which the expectations of the men regarding both the women and their society are wholly determined by their own patriarchal attitudes. They are told by the women that, shortly after their own expedition was presumed lost in space, an epidemic ravaged the earth and left the survivors genetically damaged so that no more males could be born. The women themselves are all cloned – which means that in this future the men have no function and therefore no power. Only one of the three astronauts can come to terms with this, and he is the one who throughout the narrative has been shown as having the most doubts about his masculinity. Tiptree suggests that the reactions of the men depend upon the extent to which they are fixed within the determinants of their own masculinity: thus one of the three men tries to rape a woman and engages in pornographic fantasies about being ruler over all the women. Another one invokes the patriarchal God of the Old Testament as his rationale for needing to impose his control and authority over the women, because 'women are not capable of running anything'.[6] Although the narrative is told from the point of view of the three bewildered astronauts, their inability to understand or accept this future is used to undermine their narrative 'authority'. This enables the narrative radically to question the connection between power and patriarchy. Indeed, much of the pleasure in reading this story comes from the way in which the social and sexual hierarchies governing the attitudes and behaviour of the men are satirized by the use of the narrative convention of a future women-only earth in which those hierarchies no longer make sense.

However, despite their criticism of the dominant ideology, these narratives also contain many clusters of ideas which continue to reproduce that ideology. So, while prevailing ideas about gender are clearly challenged in the narratives, the political and economic basis of those ideas is not. Class-based political transformations of society do not appear in the narratives of even those novels where there is a more explicit feminist rewriting of SF conventions, such as those by Charnas, Gearhart, and McIntyre, despite the fact that the narratives are centred on the idea that it is only through radical social change that the position of women in society will be improved. The feminist SF of the 1970s was rarely about gender *and* class, because it was gender rather than class that set the agenda for the women's movement of the 1970s. By presenting the problem of social change in terms of gender, these novels are attempting to redefine the dominant ideology, but, at the same time, by maintaining the separation of gender from politics, the narratives also reproduce that ideology. It is this contradiction that accounts for the sense of unease that is a feature of many of these texts.

Charnas's novel *Walk to the End of the World* (1974) and its sequel *Motherlines* (1979), Gearhart's novel *The Wanderground* (1976), and McIntyre's novel *Dreamsnake* (1978) all use variations on the disaster convention which involve some cataclysmic event that has profound consequences for human society.[7] This convention is a particularly useful one for allowing the social tensions and fears of the present to be extrapolated in a fairly direct way into the future. These novels take as their starting-point the way in which the violence towards women that is inherent in patriarchy has become institutionalized. In the stories by Suzy McKee Charnas, all women are slaves in the remaining cities of a post-holocaust world, but some escape from the cities to become 'free fems' and establish their own communities. Similarly, in Sally M. Gearhart's *The Wanderground*, men have absolute power over women in the cities, so women leave the cities in order to set up separate, non-hierarchical communities. The city has become the site and symbol of patriarchal brutality. Outside the cities, the women rely entirely on their own physical and psychic abilities, including the ability to reproduce without men. In Vonda McIntyre's *Dreamsnake*, society-as-we-know-it has been destroyed by some unspecified nuclear catastrophe. The city, renamed the Centre, is run by a rigid and incestuous family-centred hierarchy which prevents all outsiders from entering the Centre. To live outside the Centre means being doubly contaminated, by exposure to the effects of radiation and by not being part of the Centre's ruling family structure. McIntyre delineates the variety of individual and social groupings that are formed outside the confines of the Centre and, from a feminist perspective, explores the possibility of new kinds of social and sexual structures.

In each of these novels, the disaster convention itself has been rewritten in such a way that it is patriarchy itself which is seen as the disaster. However, that particular convention has certain resonances that cannot be ignored. Disaster novels are unavoidably deterministic because of the extrapolation of attitudes and values from the present into the future. It is a kind of determinism which is both deeply pessimistic and socially conservative because it implies a view of social and sexual relations that is based on the notion of a fixed and unchanging human nature. It is also a convention that is specifically tied to a range of anxieties about technology and social processes which, in America in the 1970s, gave rise to increasing general opposition to the political and economic consequences of corporatism, which tied in with specific demands from the emerging women's movement for social and sexual equality. These anxieties overlay the attempt to reconstitute gender relations to produce highly contradictory stories in which the utopian element is constantly undercut through the presence of a deep sense of pessimism. In Charnas's and Gearhart's novels, the most striking·thing about the societies of women is that they are constantly threatened by the 'outside' world and are therefore always unable fully to develop as coherent social alternatives. In McIntyre's novel, any changes that take place are at the level of the individual psyche, and it is a sense of social stagnation that emerges most clearly in the narrative, despite the obvious intention to present the opposite.

A writer who is acutely aware of the difficulties of writing feminist SF is Joanna Russ, whose novel *The Female Man* (1975) is justly recognized as being something of a milestone in the writing of feminist SF.[8] In the novel, Russ uses another familiar SF convention, that of the existence of parallel universes and time zones, to describe the way in which women are alienated and fragmented under patriarchy. There are four 'voices' in the novel belonging to four women from different universes. They all have similar names – Joanna, Jeannine, Janet, and Jael – and each demonstrates a different possible existence for women. Joanna inhabits a universe that is very similar to our own contemporary reality; Jeannine lives in an America where the Depression never ended and the Second World War never started; Janet comes from Whileaway, a utopian future where no men exist; and in Jael's universe the battle of the sexes has become literally war between men and women. Like the four voices, the narrative is fragmented, and the dislocations in the narrative structure undermine the 'logic' of more straightforwardly linear SF narratives and the cultural assumptions contained in them. There is neither a single plot nor a specific time sequence in the novel, and the continuous shifts from first-person to third-person narrator disrupt the familiar discursive practices of SF in a playful and witty way. The reader is given four different characters who inhabit conflicting universes with diverging political systems, and each character has a radically different perspective on her own femaleness. At the end of the novel, however, the four women come together and the narrative makes clear what has been implicit from the beginning – that they are all facets of each other, they are all 'Everywoman': 'Now you must know that Jeannine is Everywoman. I, though I am a bit quirky, I too am Everywoman. Everywoman is not Jael, as Uncle George would say – but Jael is Everywoman.'[9]

At this point, the SF convention is explicitly abandoned so that the narrative becomes something of a parody of itself. In place of a conclusion, Russ ends the narrative by referring to the material conditions of the book's existence, and this enables her to separate the feminist reading of the novel from all the other possibilities that it contains: 'Go, little book . . . and take your place bravely on the book racks of bus terminals and drug stores'.[10] The self-reflexive nature of the narrative at this point enables it to rupture the apparent ideological unity towards which it seemed to be moving once the women had been identified as different aspects of the female self. Unlike the other feminist narratives examined in this article, *The Female Man* resists narrative closure around a single ideological solution which would entail the reproduction of an essentialist view of gender. Instead, each of the four parallel universes remains a separate and distinct possibility, thus emphasizing that radical change is above all a question of making choices.

The emergence of a body of feminist science fiction in recent years demonstrates that popular narratives are an important part of the terrain of the cultural politics of feminism. It is important for a feminist cultural practice to recognize that popular narratives do not simply reproduce the dominant ideology but are involved in a constant renegotiation of those values in the dominant culture which sustain the dominant ideology. Feminist SF constantly tests the limits of that ideology by proposing alternative possibilities for social and sexual relations which are in direct conflict with existing social structures. The contradictory narratives that emerge are an indication of the complex nature of such cultural negotiations. The alternative futures of feminist science fiction provide fictional landscapes in which the reconstruction of gender can take place, and, although those landscapes are incomplete and fractured, the creation of them nevertheless represents a significant act of cultural intervention and struggle.[11]

Humberside College of Higher Education, Hull

Notes

1 A. Kolodny, 'A map for re-reading', *New Literary History*, 2 (1980), pp. 453–67.

2 See R. Brunt, 'A career in love: the romantic world of Barbara Cartland', in C. Pawling (ed.), *Popular Fiction and Social Change* (London: Macmillan, 1984); T. Modleski, *Loving with a Vengeance* (London: Methuen, 1984); J. Radway, *Reading the Romance* (Chapel Hill, NC: University of North Carolina Press, 1984).

3 Rosemary Jackson, *Fantasy: The Literature of Subversion* (London: Methuen, 1981), p. 186.

4 Isaac Asimov, *I, Robot* (London: Panther, 1968), p. 9.

5 C. J. Cherryh, *The Pride of Chanur* (London: Methuen, 1983).

6 James Tiptree, Jr, *Star Songs of an Old Primate* (New York: Ballantine, 1978), p. 220.

7 Suzy McKee Charnas, *Walk to the End of the World* (1974; London: Gollancz, 1979) and *Motherlines* (1979; London: Gollancz, 1980); Sally M. Gearhart, *The Wanderground* (1976; London: The Women's Press, 1985); Vonda McIntyre, *Dreamsnake* (1978; London: Pan, 1979).

8 Joanna Russ, *The Female Man* (1975; London: The Women's Press, 1985).

9 Ibid., p. 212.

10 Ibid., p. 213.

11 For further discussion of science fiction and feminism, see M. S. Barr (ed.), *Future Females: A Critical Anthology* (Bowling Green: Bowling Green Popular Press, 1981); E. Moers, *Literary Women* (London: The Women's Press, 1983); T. Moylan, *Demand the Impossible: Science Fiction and the Utopian Imagination* (London: Methuen, 1986); T. Staicar (ed.), *The Feminine Eye: Science Fiction and the Women Who Write It* (New York: Ungar, 1982).

MICHAEL RYAN
THE THEORY OF IDEOLOGY
RECONSIDERED

T heoretical investigations into the nature and function of ideology have been dominated for the past decade and a half by the work of Louis Althusser, indeed by one essay by this French philosopher – 'Ideology and ideological state apparatuses'.[1] It is not my purpose to rehearse here the numerous critiques of Althusser's position. I shall concentrate instead on offering an alternative, using arguments derived from deconstructive philosophy, Marxist Autonomy theory, and contemporary psychoanalysis.

The focus of the Althusserian theory of ideology is the exercise of domination through superstructural apparatuses, such as schools, the family, and culture, which enlist the participation of the oppressed in their own subjugation. Ideology makes domination voluntary, if you will. This theory of ideology can be described as Leninist. Althusser, whose work was in the service of the French Communist Party, a Leninist organization, replicates the paternalist premises of Leninism when he characterizes the masses as being duped by false consciousness and when he portrays the individual or the 'subject' as inherently ideological. The masses, in this perspective, are ideological, while the organized vanguard of the party, which can provide them with guidance, is the possessor of 'science'. This at least, I would contend, is the hidden agenda of the Althusserian theory. Moreover, the Leninist model of socialism assumes that the subject (the self or individual) is the locus of ideology because the principle of individual rights is essential to capitalism and to the social theory of liberalism which provided capitalism with legitimacy. Leninism consists of a simple inversion of the premises of liberal individualism in that it privileges the state and the party (the institutional representatives of the collectivity) over the individual. Socialist duty replaces the principle of rights. One can see why it is crucial to the Leninist project to denigrate the subject by labelling it as ideological. Around that definition cluster certain very important political stakes, most important of which perhaps is the promotion of the belief that self-denial and self-sacrifice are 'socialist' ideals. Socialism consists of the annulment of the self into the collective. And that collective will be guided by an élite who possess privileged access to science. Thus the theoretical description of social history as a 'process without a subject' which is held back by an essentially subjective ideology contains a political agenda which is not at first evident but which is inscribed in Althusser's very categories.

That Althusser's theory of ideology is Leninist tends to be ignored by its current practitioners. That it might not even be 'Marxist', in the sense of deriving from Marx's work and fitting into the general principles outlined in his work, is never interrogated. Perhaps the most important of those principles is the idea of the dialectic of subject and object, of subjective power and objective transformation independent of subjective force, in the development of society. Human labour power creates the social world – that is the basic assumption of all Marxist politics. The notion of a 'process without a subject' (to name social history) is therefore quite antithetical to the spirit of Marx's texts, as is the assumption that the subject is inherently ideological. Marx suggested just the opposite, in fact. Ideology, in his view, consisted of the attempt to annul the role human subjective activity played in the construction of the world through recourse to abstract idealist and objectivist or positivist descriptions. Abstract transcendental principles like 'freedom' turned the materiality of human labour into concepts which misrepresented that materiality; the utilitarian calculus transmuted human relations of domination into a spuriously objective logic of reality; and the pervasive use of natural metaphors in liberal social theory denied the human-made world its subjectively constructed and historical character. If Marx did attack subjectivity, it was the subjective idealism of certain religiously minded philosophers, but that subjectivism has little to do with the material subjectivity of actual human activity.

The Leninist and Althusserian identification of ideology with subjectivity is most at odds with Marx in its implied programme for a post-capitalist society. A negative description always implies a positive alternative. To call the subject ideological is to point towards a subject-less, non-ideological society. Communism would consist of universal self-annulment. This, again, is quite different from what Marx had in mind when he described communism as the fulfilment of subjective creative power, the liberation of a temporality in which full human development could occur without any of the restraints imposed by capitalism. If anything, communism would be the realization of subjectivity, not its annulment. It should not be surprising that the very books where Marx makes these arguments (the early manuscripts, the *Grundrisse*) are precisely the ones which Leninists like Althusser declare to be non-canonical. If Leninism consists of such a radical inversion of the basic premises of Marx's text, then it scarcely merits being called 'Marxist', and the same can be said of a Leninist theory of ideology like the one Althusser proposes. Leninism replaces a democratic and egalitarian ideal with an élitist and hierarchical model of party guidance. Althusser's Leninist theory of ideology legitimates that very non-Marxist political programme, whereby the masses would be led by an élite of scientific seers. That Marx made scalding fun of such nonsense in the nineteenth century should perhaps alert us to the appropriate attitude of scepticism with which it should be greeted in the twentieth.

The Leninist interpretation of Marx lies under Althusser's theory of ideology, but other interpretations exist, and they programme different theories of ideology. One such alternative interpretation was offered by Antonio Negri and others in Italy in the 1970s who participated in what was called the 'Autonomy' movement.[2] That movement argued that workers did not need to wait for party directives in order to revolt; the workers, not the party, were the real locus of revolutionary activity. While Leninists argued that workers' economic struggles need to be guided and mediated by a political institution like the party, the Autonomy theorists argued that economic struggles were immediately political. Workers possessed power over capital by virtue of their position as the real creators of social wealth. Therefore, their political programme should be elaborated at the site of production itself, not through the mediation of the party. Their ability to control their work (or to refuse work outright; hence the slogan 'zerowork') was itself a political weapon, one which could not be directed from above by party bureaucrats, who tended to sell out workers in order to guarantee their own political legitimacy. The basic premise of the movement was that capitalist work was itself a form of oppression. The Leninist parties merely offered a continuation of such work under the title of 'socialism'. Workers would learn to sacrifice to the state and the party – while continuing to work, that is, to be exploited. Only a theory like Autonomy, which located political oppression in the work form itself and which saw labour as itself a political force, could transcend this continuity between capitalism and Leninist socialism. Against the Leninists, it insisted that economic relations were fundamentally relations of political domination, not neutral and objective institutions which could continue under a different name as socialism. It is obvious why the Leninist theory of ideology might appear objectionable from an autonomist perspective, since it denies any reality to subjectivity, and it programmes precisely the sort of self-sacrifice which Leninist socialism always demands of workers, whose needs must be deferred and whose power must be denied in the name of the right of the party to lead. The Leninist/Althusserian theory of ideology is thus linked to a politics which seeks to control the autonomist impulses of workers, their tendency to seek liberation from a situation of oppression, be it called capitalism or socialism.

The theorists of Autonomy were thus distinctly non-Leninist, although they did not dismiss Lenin entirely. They promoted a more radical perception of the power of the popular base, the level of material need and desire which Althusserians dismiss as 'imaginary'. The argued that capitalism could be overcome only when the oppressed (not just factory workers – the core of the Leninist party – but all 'social workers', including the unemployed and 'houseworkers') came to place their own needs, their own desires for value and self-worth, before the profit prerequisites of the economic system. 'Self-valorization', not self-denial (as in the Leninist model), should be the motor of a Marxist revolutionary politics, in economics as in culture. This strategy of resistance is simultaneously an ideal of a post-capitalist society of the sort Marx describes in the *Grundrisse*, one in which the producers of social wealth would directly appropriate their product in a way which would liberate them from wage labour entirely and generate a society of free time given over to the development of multiple subjective possibilities. Communism in this autonomist sense does not consist of an absorption of the subject into a party-directed unfolding of the logic of history, the 'process without a subject'. Nor does it entail self-sacrifice for the state. Rather, it is something that arises out of the material process of subjective development and expression; communism is the possibility of full individual and collective self-development within a co-operative and communal social arrangement.

Negri argues that the productive potential harboured in subjective creative activity works against the limits on production which capital must impose if profitability is to be maintained. Profits drop if too many goods glut the market, and workers must be rendered unemployed to rectify the situation. Negri sees the 'crisis of overproduction' as a testament to the potential for a sufficiently high level of production to make communism possible. His argument is that communism is not some future goal towards which history moves inexorably or logically (as in the Leninist Communist Party theory of 'capital logic'); rather, communism is an inherent possibility within capitalism which is contained and prevented from emerging. Subjective energy, the power to create, is thus a political principle; capital is a perverse constraint on a force which is responsible for creating the existing social world and which moves towards the creation of an altogether different world, one in which overproduction would be the criterion of the universal satisfaction of needs and desires. Capital restrains this possibility through recourse to spuriously objective economic mechanisms of political control. This, in fact, is the point where ideology comes into play as the denial of subjectivity, the replacement of a recognition of the fact that the economy is a site of political contention between two subjects with descriptions which suggest that inflation, unemployment, and so on, are merely the working out of an objective logic. Ideology in this sense consists of saying that capitalism is a machine which humans cannot control, that the social world is not in the power of the subjects who create it, and that human labour is an objectively necessary component of a system, rather than a form of political slavery which is central to capitalism. The theory of Autonomy argues that everything that seems objective in the development of capitalism is the result of the political struggle between the two subjects which comprise the process – capital and labour. The critique of ideology thus consists of a restoration of the sense of the subjective make-up of the seemingly objective social world. If ideology is its denial, the transcendence of ideology consists of the affirmation of the power of subjectivity.

It is easy to imagine why Autonomy might have attracted the ire of a Leninist Italian Communist Party which sought to control the workers' movement, to limit its scope, and to direct its activities. Autonomy constituted both a theoretical and a practical challenge to Leninist power and to the Leninist monopoly on what counted as 'Marxism'. Many of the leaders of the movement ended up in prison, with the full blessing of the followers of Gramsci. And even anglophone Gramscian Leninists attempt to write the moment of Autonomy off the map of Marxist history entirely. Perry Anderson, in his book *In the Tracks of Historical Materialism*,[3] argues that there has been no Marxist writing on political strategy in the past two decades, when in fact during the seventies Negri did nothing but write on Marxist political strategy, in such books as *Proletarians and the State*, *Domination and Sabotage*, and *Communism and War*.

This 'alternative' Marxism suggests the possibility of a non-Leninist theory of ideology, one which would accord a greater power to subjectivity and which would not adopt a dismissive and élitist attitude towards the mass of people. Indeed, just as one can see capital in the light of Autonomy theory as having constantly to respond to workers' struggles for greater actual and social wages and power, so also one can reconceptualize ideology as a response to needs, desires, and forces which, if they were not channelled and contained, would threaten to tear apart the society of domination from inside. Similarly, the conservative Lacanian psychoanalytic model which supplies the Leninist theory of ideology with grounds for describing the ego as 'imaginary' can also be reconceptualized along parallel lines. It privileges structure over self in a reprise of some of the more right-wing forms of existentialism, and it can be rewritten using more up-to-date psychoanalytic insights which suggest greater possibilities for political change.

The Althusserian theory of ideology holds that domination is the primary focus of analysis, but one could as easily argue that ideology is a secondary term, a response to other factors which may be more worthy of analysis simply because they might be the sites of positive political possibilities. One could argue that ideology is itself made necessary by the tensions that arise around the structural inequalities of a white-run, patriarchal, capitalist society like the USA; by the possibility that those who work rather than own, those who are the real producers of the material wealth of the society, possess the power to overthrow the system of exploitation; and by the antinomies, the unresolvable aporias, of a social system founded on irrational principles which must conceal the truth of its operation from those it exploits. These persistent and irreducible forces are what are contained and kept at bay by ideology. Ideology in this perspective is less the determinant of public consciousness, a free exercise of power, than a defensive operation, a response to factors that, were they not pacified, would tear the society apart from inside. Ideology is an exercise in power, but it is also a response to the power of forces that, were they not channelled in ways conducive to the hegemony of whites, males, and capitalists, would push the society towards an altogether different sort of arrangement, one potentially antithetical to the interests of those in power. I am assuming here that structures of inequality tend towards equalization by virtue of their own forces and tensions, and that ideology is an attempt to prevent that from happening. For this reason, I see ideology less as a positive vector of domination than as a negative attempt to prevent the inevitable from occurring. In other words, ideology prevents certain things from being known, but it also prevents certain things from occurring; its being is defined by an 'anti-ideology', another world altogether that it prevents from coming into being, a world that would turn this one inside out.

Ideology can thus be read as a symptom of the very thing ideology acts to conjure away – the potential for a radical inversion of structural inequality. By attempting to pacify, channel, and displace the forces that would generate such an inversion were they not neutralized, ideology testifies to the power of the very thing it denies. Inequality and oppression create an irreducible structural tension that makes ideology necessary as a response, but which remains immune to the therapeutic operation of ideology. Therefore, ideological artefacts can serve as good barometers of the potentials for radical change in a society. By reacting against those structural tensions and those potentially disruptive forces in a way that renders them invisible, they must also simultaneously put them on display.

For these reasons, ideology requires a double reading. On the one hand, it discloses the way in which desire and fear are channelled to assure hegemony. On the other hand, it also provides a measure of those forces that threaten to overturn hegemony. Even conservative artefacts, therefore, can yield socially critical insights, for what they designate in a sort of inverse negative is the presence of forces that make conservative reactions necessary. The monologue of power invariably turns out to be a dialogue.

This critique assumes that ideology is an antidote, and that a critical method that merely records how successfully the antidote works fails to account for why it was needed in the first place. A deconstructive approach seeks out what in society makes ideology necessary at all. Generally, ideology sets up boundaries which establish 'proper' domains that are part of a broader social system of ordering or 'propriety' that is integral to the exercise of power. For example, it is proper that liberal notions of equality and rights should not be allowed to penetrate the economy, which must, under liberal capitalism, be reserved as a feudal domain characterized by relations of domination. Similarly, the liberal public-sphere notions of contract and obligation must not be permitted to penetrate the private sphere of family life, which, under patriarchy, is deemed uncontaminated by the liberal principles of contract and the necessity of legislated equality. The deconstructive analysis of ideology uncovers the intermediation of realms that ideology keeps apart – culture and politics, sexuality and public policy, psychology and economics, and so on. If economic pressure has negative psychological effects on workers, so also the principle of capitalist competition derives or 'refers to' sexual power as its operative principle. If politics 'refers to' culture for its substance, culture is inseparable from the political distribution of cultural goods. Deconstruction suggests that material forces are at work – signalled by the flow of reference from one domain to another and beyond – which undermine from within the ideological boundaries that help maintain social power. Consequently, using deconstructive analysis, one can go beyond the usual charting of successful domination in the critique of ideology and ask instead what aspects of ideology point towards the reconstruction of society along progressive lines, not on the basis of a utopian aspiration for another world, but on the basis of immanent or inherent and incipient possibilities within this world. For what these deconstructive possibilities suggest is that real forces are at work which threaten the boundaries that ideology stabilizes. Those possibilities can be flushed out through a recharacterization of the psychoanalytic schema which underlies the theory of ideology.

Althusser's theory of ideology is buttressed by Lacan's negative psycho-analytic definition of human subjectivity. The ego is 'imaginary', prone to narcissistic self-identifications which blind it to its determination by unconscious and instinctual processes. In the history of the psychoanalytic movement, Lacan's work represents a conservative restoration, an attempt to roll back advances towards a more radical theory of the social constructedness of the self and to re-establish the ascendancy of the late Freud's pessimistic and anti-progressive vision of human nature. Yet, just as more politically enabling non-Leninist Marxist models are available as the basis for an alternative theory of ideology, so also more politically promising psychoanalytic models can be found. Contemporary psychoanalytic theory underscores the role of representation in the construction of the self, in a manner which emphasizes both the continuity between culture and psychology and the constructed character of the psyche. Psychic maturation and health are foremost a matter of developing a capacity for mental representation. And certain forms of mental dysfunction such as schizophre-nia have come to be seen as consisting in part of a failure to develop such a capacity. Representation is important because it allows the person to mark out boundaries between the self and the world as well as between objects in the world. At the earliest stages of development, representation enables the child to tolerate separation from initial caretakers; by representing them to herself in their absence, the child can learn to accept the sense of loss that separation entails. The capacity to form an autonomous self is thus predicated on the ability to represent. If that initial separation is executed successfully – that is, if it is represented in a manner that avoids distress – then the child is likely to continue to develop a capacity to represent the world in a way which is not neurotic, and to build a self which is capable of relating without needing to fuse and capable of autonomy without exaggerated defensiveness. Neurotic representation is either too indistinct or too distinct; it erects excessive representational boundaries between objects or between self and world which are designed to protect a vulnerable self, or it has trouble constructing representational boundaries, with the result that the self is excessively oriented toward fusion with others.[4] The political correlates of these problems are the radical individualist philosophy of 'freedom' without social responsibility (contemporary conservative ideol-ogy) and the authoritarian philosophy of fascist fusion in a unified and orderly social corporation.

Representations are also taken from the culture and internalized, adopted as part of the self. When internalized, they mould the self in such a way that it becomes accommodated to the values inherent in those cultural represen-tations. Consequently, the sort of representations which prevail in a culture is a crucial political issue. Cultural representations not only give shape to psychological dispositions; they also play an important role in determining how social reality will be constructed – that is, what figures and boundaries will prevail in the shaping of social life and social institutions. Representations give structure and shape to social life and determine the substance and form of the everyday world. For example, the discourse of technocratic capitalism, with its ideals of progress and modernization, embodies certain material interests, but it also consists of representations which shape and transform the social world. Indeed, one could say that the very substance of capitalist modernity depends on such representations; it could not exist without them. The ideal of 'progress' is a metaphor, a figure which allows specific economic interests to be transported across class lines and universalized, while also underwriting the reshaping of material life. The same can be said of people's social roles and psychological dispositions in a capitalist culture. Businessmen live by one set of representations, housewives by another. The prevailing cultural representations that shape a businessman's life prescribe certain patterns of behaviour, thought, and feeling, and set boundaries over which he cannot cross. Similarly, the housewife internalizes representations which prescribe a quite different set of attitudes and habits, different boundaries on thought and action. The acceptance of such boundaries or limitations constitutes one's life as a synecdoche, a part which stands in for a whole, in that one allows one's life possibilities to be curtailed, reduced to a part, in order to fulfil a function in the larger whole of technocratic capitalist social life. One's being is thus shaped by the representations of oneself and of the world that one holds, and one's life can be described in terms of the figures or shapes which social life assumes as a result of the representations that prevail in a culture.

The political stakes of control over the production of cultural representations are thus very high indeed. But the insight contemporary psychoanalytic theory permits into the essential role that representation plays in constructing both the self and the social world also opens up more radical possibilities than were allowed by the Lacanian approach. Seen as a construct made from internalized representation, the self becomes more amenable to change and reconstruction. By contrast with the Lacanian approach, which places more importance on unchanging drives which are not at all determined by social relations and which consequently cannot be reconstructed, this approach suggests that all dimensions of the psyche, even those which are supposedly unconscious, primary, or instinctual, are historical and social, that is, malleable.

Moreover, this shift in psychoanalytic perspective suggests that ideology is not a matter of an opposition between false consciousness or subjectivity and objective 'science' (as in the Althusserian theory). It is rather a matter of representations which shape human subjects and the social world in different ways. Consequently, the form of representation becomes a crucial focus of the critique of ideology. Indeed, form of representation comes to be seen as what constitutes ideological consciousness and ideological social institutions. Psychoanalytic testing has shown that more resolved and differentiated mental representations correspond to greater levels of non-neurotic psychological functioning.[5] Since conservatism is characterized by both excessive fusion and excessive individualism, one could say that conservatism is marked by lower, less resolved and differentiated, representational capacities. Because conservatives represent themselves and the world in a certain way, or because they lack certain capacities of representation, they tend to seek political forms which are themselves the embodiment of representations which promote fusion, or authority, or extreme individualism. The critique of ideology, then, is not simply a matter of debunking false consciousness in the name of a science of true or real representations. It is a matter of developing alternative representational forms which are more differentiated and resolved, permitting both autonomy and relation at once. And this formal concern is necessarily linked to institutional reconstruction, since these forms of representation are also immediately matters of living different family forms, desiring different political forms, and so on. To understand the power of ideology and to foresee its displacement, it is necessary to grasp this nexus where subjectivity and social institutions are welded together by representation.

The Althusserian theory of ideology has not proved to be politically enabling. But it was never meant to be. Written by a man who himself and whose political party assumed an essentially counter-revolutionary position in 1968, it is a theory which permits almost no leeway for mobilizations which emerge from the popular base. The alternative theory I have proposed allows for an understanding of ideology which incorporates such mobilization as one of its fundamental premises. Ideology, I have argued, must be seen as a response to incipient possibilities, latent movements which are necessarily inscribed in a society of inequality. Such a society is a temporary stabilization of forces in tension, and those forces tend towards a running down or equalization. Ideology counters this possibility by justifying that temporary stabilization, but it is therefore necessarily marked by the forces it deflects. It is a testament to counter-power, even as it reaffirms power. Similarly, as representations which shape subjectivity and the commonly held sense of social reality, ideology testifies to desires and needs which are potentially counter-hegemonic. The psychoanalytic alternative to Lacan which I propose emphasizes the contingent and indeterminate character of those needs and desires. They are inseparable from representations; to fear or desire is to bear a relation to a mental representation of what is feared or desired. The prevailing cultural representations, when internalized, shape those feelings into ideology, into modes of thought and action appropriate to the maintaining of domination. But those feelings are not themselves ideological. It is at this point that the deconstructive slant of my critique assumes its full applicability, for what it would suggest is that no inherent meaning can be assigned to the sorts of subjective dispositions which Althusser sees as being ideological. Those dispositions are constituted by representations, and they can be remade by representations. What this points to is the necessity of a politics of representation on the popular level.

The Althusserian position programmes an élitist favouring of pseudo-scientific reflexivity in left cultural work which disdains popular representational forms. The presupposition of this approach was that such forms are indelibly ideological. I would suggest, rather, that popular representation is something to be struggled over. And it is necessary to engage in such struggle because, as contemporary psychoanalytic theory suggests, which representations prevail in a culture determine to a large degree the political possibilities for change in that society.

Northwestern University, Boston, Massachusetts

Notes

1 Louis Althusser, 'Ideology and ideological state apparatuses', in *Lenin and Philosophy* (London: New Left Books, 1971), pp. 127–88.
2 For an account of Negri's work, see M. Ryan, 'The theory of Autonomy in the works of Antonio Negri', in A. Negri, *Marx Beyond Marx*, trans. H. Cleaver, M. Ryan, and M. Viano (Amherst: Bergin, 1984). The book also includes a bibliography. See also T. Negri and F. Guattari, *The New Politics* (New York: Semiotext(e), 1986).
3 P. Anderson, *In the Tracks of Historical Materialism* (London: Verso, 1983).
4 See especially R. Schafer, *Aspects of Internalization* (New York: International Universities Press, 1968), and G. Platte and F. Weinstein, *Psychoanalytic Sociology* (Baltimore: Johns Hopkins University Press, 1972). See also D. Beres and E. Joseph, 'The concept of mental representation in psychoanalysis', *International Journal of Psychoanalysis*, 51 (1970), pp. 1–9; S. J. Blatt and S. Shichman, 'Two primary configurations of psychopathology', *Psychoanalysis and Contemporary Thought*, 6, 2 (1983), pp. 187–254; S. J. Blatt, 'Levels of object representation in anaclitic and introjective depression', *Psychoanalytic Study of the Child*, 29 (1974), pp. 107–57; S. J. Blatt, C. Wild, and B. Ritzler, 'Disturbances of object representation in schizophrenia', *Psychoanalysis and Contemporary Science*, 4 (1975), pp. 235–88; S. Fraiberg, 'Libidinal object constancy and mental representation', *Psychoanalytic Study of the Child*, 24 (1969), pp. 9–47; L. Freedman, 'The barren prospect of a representational world', *Psychoanalytic Quarterly*, 39 (1980), pp. 215–33; A. Loewald, 'On internalization', *International Journal of Psychoanalysis*, 54 (1973), pp. 9–17; A. Loewald, 'Instinct theory, object relations, and psychic structure formation', *Journal of the American Psychoanalytic Association*, 29 (1978), pp. 39–106; P. Noy, 'Symbolism and mental representation', *International Review of Psychoanalysis*, 2 (1975), pp. 171–87.
5 See S. Blatt, J. Schimek, and B. Brenneis, 'The nature of psychotic experience and its implications for the therapeutic process', in J. Strauss *et al.* (eds), *Psychotherapy of Schizophrenia* (New York: Plenum, 1980), and the entries in note 4 above.

UNTITLED: (ON GENRE)

I

W hen the title 'Untitled' started appearing beneath paintings, it corresponded to the claim of abstract painting to be non-representational: to be 'painting', simply – just as we have learnt to say, more recently in literature, 'writing', and, with Beckett, 'Film'. It is a title that represents the non-representational. Now, since the titles of paintings – place-names, personal names, the names of historical or legendary events, or kinds of subjects – designate not only their represented subjects but also, through the naming conventions themselves, their genres, the title 'Untitled' claims above all to transcend genre. Reflect on this. For 'untitled' paintings are themselves a genre; and the title 'Untitled' points to genre in the very act of its denial. It is metageneric, inextricably implicated in and implicating the problem of kinds in its spectacular failure to not-classify.

II

My father put a hex on me, one day, when he was trying for the nth time to teach me to hit tennis-balls against the wall of the back lav. He told me I had no ball sense. What he meant, of course, was what we nowadays call hand–eye co-ordination, and I've since learnt to separate the issues. But it's had untold consequences. One is that tennis can never be more, or less, for me than a metaphor. Or maybe I mean a simile. Or an allegory.

Imagine a game of tennis, preferably, of course (if you have any ball sense), singles. The players are not exchanging balls, they're exchanging shots. The ball, like the rackets, the players themselves, the court with its markings, and the rules of the game, is one of the things that make the shots possible. Without the ball, and with everything else, the shots are possible but not realized. Even this problem has been solved for board games, such as chess, but only by means of the ingenious invention of material substitutes for the board and the men ('men', in chess, includes the queen). As Saussure said,

Parts II and III of this paper originally appeared as parts 1 and 2 of a paper entitled 'Anyone for tennis?', in Ian Reid (ed.), *The Place of Genre in Learning: Current Debates*, Typereader Publications no. 1, Centre for Studies in Literary Education (Deakin University, 1987), pp. 91–124.

any substitute for the piece will work exactly like the piece, if the rules governing its piece-hood (its manhood?) are spelled out. The material determinants of tennis-balls are more intractable: you need another tennis-ball, though children make do with almost anything.

Let us take the distinction between exchanging balls and exchanging shots as something like the distinction between 'exchanging meanings' and 'exchanging signs' respectively. I expect you thought I should have made an equivalence between 'ball' and 'sign', and between 'shot' and 'meaning'. This shot is about why I didn't. Imagine hard little pellets of meaning travelling towards you like a Mandlikovan serve. Then duck. Michael Reddy calls this 'the conduit metaphor'.[1]

If we said, about tennis or any other ball game, that what we were exchanging was the ball, scoring would not be possible. The game would be posited on the absolute symmetry of the players, and its objective, if objective there were in such circumstances, would be its maintenance. There are games in which the confirmation of balance is the only stake, and the loss of balance a sign that the match should not have taken place. I heard, for instance, of a betrothal ritual from the Cameroons. In it, the fathers of the prospective couple enter into an intellectual joust, where they match their respective funds of cultural knowledge and skill. They argue for as long as they are well matched, and a ritual ending marking neither victory nor defeat proclaims that the match is a good one. Winning becomes important in a situation such as this only if one of the protagonists, with his seconds, begins to lose respect in a systematic or protracted way for his opposite number; then he must win, to demonstrate publicly that inequality was the proven outcome; the marriage then will not take place. This is not unlike the system of 'seeding' in championship tennis: any one match between top seeds may be won or lost, where the understanding is that the result could reverse at the next round. The contrast with the single singles match is not, after all, so great: in any given match, winning is what the players are trying to do, though they must be well matched for the game to be worth playing; while, in the most ritual of jousts and the most equal of display games, equality, no less than winning and losing, depends on scoring. Scoring depends on shots, not on balls.

Player A plays a shot; player B plays it back. What is this 'it'? It is not useful to say '"it" is the ball'; and it is manifestly inaccurate to call it the same shot. Player B is, let's say, the 'receiver', but to *receive* a shot she or he must return it – play, that is to say, another. The same shot, then (player A's serve), has a *different value* for each of the two players: a 'good shot' may win a point for its player, but, well received, it may turn against him or her, its speed, its turn, or its angle enabling an unexpected return.

If I return, now, to the silent comparand, you may well wish to object that we have always known this, that words or texts have different meanings for any two interlocutors, that it's what we do with them that counts. So I'd best not return, just yet. If tennis is to be a simile, it had better pay off better than that.

One of the arguments we've been having recently, in literary theory/theory of discourse/theory of text/linguistics, is whether, grossly, the meaning is governed 'by the text' or 'by the reading'. Structuralist poetics was supposed to be discredited for claiming that the meaning was 'in the text', and entirely governed by the rules of the code. So along came the varieties of pragmatics and reception theory, to say that it was 'in the reader' or, less naïvely, in the reading. The objection to structuralist poetics was that, if you said it was 'in the text', this was tantamount to remobilizing authorial intentions as embodied in a piece of writing, and to claiming that reading was the surrender of self discussed by phenomenological criticism as the ethics of the reading attitude. A simple translation of this on to the tennis-courts would have player B receiving but not returning the ball, quite possibly caressing it, and asking for the video replay immediately so he or she could contemplate in tranquillity the way in which it came to him or her. A simple translation of the other side of the same story would have player A (anon.), playing without a partner, back to the wall.

What counts as 'structuralism' in this argument is a use made of structuralist poetics by the American New Criticism, which shored up what it had always done with a bit of second-hand linguistics. Structuralist poetics is different from this in a crucial respect: it replaced the concept 'meaning' with the concept 'value', and meant by 'value' what Saussure had meant – that is, the differential place/role/function of a piece/sign in the system to which it belongs. What has happened to that notion, more recently, is that we say that the value of a sign is continually being renegotiated by its use and usage. To suppose the value as given and fixed by the code is not very different from meaning 'meaning' with a new name. Remember those little pellets. To suppose that discursive interaction is the giving and receiving of *meanings* is like describing a game of tennis as the giving and receiving of balls. To suppose, on the contrary, that it is the playing of shots is to allow the value of those shots to be subject to play, and the meaning of the interaction to be the upshot of the perpetual modification of each shot by its return.

Each shot, in this analogy, produces value in two ways: in what it enables, or prevents; and to either player. Each shot is formally determined by the rules of the game, and materially determined by the skill of the players, and each return shot is determined by the shot to which it is a response. Responses, then, are not 'free', or bound even by what is loosely known as pragmatic circumstance as if this latter were 'outside' the text. Returns, and readings, work within certain clearly marked conventions, and *with the material at hand*. They are both enabled and constrained by the formal-material determinants of the signs they read and the signs they will write.

Our signs, then, our semiotic artefacts, bid for value in a field of like and unlike; and their value as objects resides neither 'in' them nor in their owners. Rather, using the analogy of the market-place – the extent to which they are kept in play (the number of times they are bid for, the changes they effect around them, the bids they make for place and function within this field) – they have no value if they are not constantly renegotiated. Priceless, they say, of paintings, and of conversation-stopping jokes.

So . . . maybe . . . then . . . too . . . (if I go on) . . . (*allons, Gogo, il faut me renvoyer la balle de temps en temps*) . . . a metaphor, a simile, or an allegory is just this: the play of a sign between two systems of values, itself an allegory, of what it is to play ball, or to make sense.

III

What is the value of this very elaborate metaphor, you may well ask. It seems to have worked well enough as a way of writing about Communication, or Discourse, and it is tempting to take the metaphor of a *game* to correspond with the notion of 'genre'. The authority for this usage is Wittgenstein.[2] Yet there is little evidence in his use of the metaphor of the 'language game' that it designates in his writings a concept commensurate with that conventionally associated with 'genre'. The kind of thing meant by 'language game' might be, for example, 'referring', or 'asking questions', and could be said to *overlap* with that of 'genre' to the extent that 'genre' is either modelled on, or thought through, the concept of the *speech act*. Literary theorists, and linguists concerned with discourse, have been led, quite fruitfully, to consider genre as an extension of speech acts, and have, accordingly, attempted to construct *theories of genre* that extend *the theory of speech acts*.[3] Historians of what we are wont to call ideas argue that there is a great deal in common between the Wittgensteinian notion of the 'language game' and the theory of speech acts deriving from Austin.[4] Both, they would say, are strategies for contesting the dominance of the formal models used by logic to describe meaning. They would also say that this move in philosophy is paralleled by the move in literary theory which has adopted pragmatic notions of *discourse as social action* to contest formal models of textuality,[5] or the more traditional notion that the meaning of a text resides solely in its 'referential function', i.e. what it can be said to represent. In all these places, discourse is conceived in terms of 'doing things with words', and terms like 'perform', 'function', 'act', 'action', 'moves', 'strategies', 'tactics', and so on, figure large in such theories. Since a lot of this vocabulary is common to the ways in which we talk about playing games and how we talk about our engagement in social forms and forces, it is tempting to talk about *a genre* as if it were *a game*. It seems to suggest a combination of the serious and the playful, and to authorize the use of the model of constitutive rules (as in the description of games) with the need to talk about individual action in relation to regulative rules (as in the description of social facts). The authority for this combination is Searle,[6] who in many ways combines Wittgensteinian notions (e.g. taking 'referring' as an act) with the impetus given to speech-act theory by Austin.

However, 'the game' – or, rather, *a game* – may be a misleading metaphor for genre. It may require some adjustment. It suggests that once you have learnt the rules – implicit and explicit, and including rules such as those that constitute the basis of skill (e.g. one's grip in golf or tennis) – the playing of a correct game follows automatically, like the output from a simple algorithmic programme in a computer. Obviously individual variables such as actual skill, mental and physical agility, and so on, play a part, but they are not an issue if what is at stake is whether what you are doing *counts as* the playing of that game. To use this metaphor for genre suggests that a text is the output of a set of rules. This is what I call the 'recipe theory' of genre. We have known for many years that a very wide range of 'texts' – far beyond what usually pass for 'literary', 'artistic', or 'creative' texts – fail to be usefully described as conforming with a generic recipe; we have also known for many years that it is this kind of genre theory with its failures that has caused the discrediting of the very notion of genre, bringing about in turn its disuse and the disrepair many of us found it in, within the last, say, five to ten years, when we attempted to apply it to the emerging set of problems in literary and semiotic theory. What constitutes a game as distinct from other games is its rules, their rules, and the difference between them. This is important. But we need to adjust our metaphor to accommodate the idea that these rules are *rules for play*.

In the description of the game of tennis I gave in part II, I described the playing of a shot in terms that converge in the notion of 'uptake'. This may be said to correspond to the 'tactical' level of game-playing; on this analogy, the 'strategic' level corresponds to the attempt to determine the terms in which the interaction – the game – is set up. 'Uptake' is a term from speech-act theory, and it is said that kinds of speech acts (requests, commands, invitations, and so on) determine the (set of) appropriate uptake(s). The strategic level of game-playing is that level where a (set of) medium-term goal(s) is established, and the tactics planned in accordance with this. It is the relation between strategy and tactics that suggests that genre might be a generalization over speech acts, or an extension of the notion. But it is also this relation that shows us that we are no longer talking about a game and its rules; we are talking about the playing of a game. In the very elaborate discussion of chess strategies, so formalized that they take on the status of *kinds of games*, there is no discussion of the relation of these strategies with the tactics of the play at any given point, except in the detailed descriptions of particular matches. You might just as well substitute 'particular texts', in the previous sentence. Now the playing of a game is a *ceremony* which involves a great deal more than the game itself. There are the preparations, the choice of partners, occasion, and venue. There is the warm-up, the toss, and, at the end, the declaration of the winner and the closing-down rituals – showers, presentations, or the drink at the bar.

There may be no important ethnographic or sociological difference between the notion of a ceremonial and that of a game, but I need to retain the two terms for tactical purposes. Ceremonies are games that situate other games: they are the rules for the setting of a game, for constituting participants as players in that game, for placing and timing it in relation to other places and times. They are the rules for the playing of a game, but they are not the rules of the game. Games, then, are rules for the production of certain acts in those 'places'. To the extent that the grammatical rules of my language permit me to make this distinction, I could say that, where ceremonies are rules for playing, games are rules of play. That there is 'play' at both these levels is important: knowing the rules is knowing what would break the rules, but being a skilled player is knowing how much play the rules allow and how to play with them. I want to suggest, then, that each of the moments, phases, stages, or 'places' in a ceremonial is a genre, and that speech acts might have the function of the opening or closing of the ceremony, the marking of the passage from one phase to another, as well as of tactics 'within' any genre. If this is the case, the notion of genre and the notion of speech act are not co-extensive, and are not usefully thought of as deriving one from the other. I also want to suggest that it will be useful to think of most of our talking and writing as ceremonial, and that what we can mean, in the semiotics of discourse, by 'social setting' can be usefully explored by means of this series of analogies.

There are points of similarity between the framework I am setting up and the Hallidayan model of register.[7] Schematically, on the assumption that games are formalized symbolic structurings of interlocutory relations, then field : tenor :: ceremonial : game. My terminology has the advantage of declaring the kind of relation that might hold between the two 'levels', but this may not be a difference worth fighting over. On the other hand, there are significant differences between the two models. Mine is a model in general semiotics, which starts from the postulate that 'texts' are the product of the interaction of a variety of 'languages', or semiotic systems, none necessarily homologous with any other. The Hallidayan model and its derivates arise from the postulate of a functionalist linguistics, which maps social structures into the single semiotic system we call 'natural language' or 'human discourse'. The argument for the general semiotics position is that it is practically impossible to find a text that mobilizes only one language: the relation of speech and gestures is the most immediately available example of this claim; the relation of typesetting and other publishing conventions with the 'written' forms of language is another. In this perspective, film is not an exception to this semiotic rule but a particularly rich exploitation of it. The limitations of linguistic models of, or premises for, a theory of discourse arise quite naturally from the theoretical and methodological enterprise of linguistics itself. The argument against the linguistic models is, then, that if we are to account for what it is to make a text we are unlikely to find out a great deal from studying the properties of only one of its languages.

There is another difference between my position and that of the linguists with respect to the more precise question of genre; but the problem I wish to raise is not in this case a direct product of the premises of linguistics. Rather, I am taking issue with the whole tradition of genre theory as it derives from literary studies. Most unfortunately, it seems that the linguists have taken over some tacit assumptions from this tradition and have fallen into the 'traps for young players' that recent literary theory has attempted to undo. Briefly, these assumptions are:

1 that a text is 'in' a genre, i.e. that it is primarily, or solely, describable in terms of the rules of one genre;
2 that genre is 'in' a text, i.e. that the features of a text will correspond to the rules of the genre.

If, as I am suggesting, a genre is the ceremonial placing of discursive acts, then it will be more useful to think of it as consisting, minimally, of two texts, in some sort of dialogical relation. For example:

theoretical debate;
brief and report;
play and audience response;
essay question, essay, and feedback.

Some of these will be in the same ceremonial, and others will be in distinct ones, for example:

a recipe and its making, and the meal.

Sometimes the insertion of a text into an inappropriate ceremonial will make for parody (as Malcolm Muggeridge is said to have said, 'How better could you parody this letter [which appeared in *The Times*] than by reprinting it verbatim in *Punch*?'), but at other times such misappropriation just makes nonsense, or at best restates or recuperates the borrowed text in the terms of the borrowing ceremonial. For example, the use of simulation techniques in the ceremonial frame of 'straight' classroom practice subverts the simulated game: its stakes are no longer at stake; the stakes of playing are those of playing the usual work-for-marks-and-teacher's-feedback game. What has gone wrong is that the pairing of the text produced by the simulation with its appropriate uptake has been broken. It has simply become another assignment.

If genres are usefully described as pairs or groups of texts, certain implications follow:

1 texts, like speech acts, are tactical;
2 the rules of a genre, and the formal properties of a single text, will not correlate; but rather
3 the two texts of a generic pair will have different properties, like question and answer, theory and refutation;
4 one of the things a text will do is to play its partner, whether or not that partner is 'present'. In order to do so, it must *represent* its partner – previous, current, future, fictional, or ideal. The rules for such representations are an integral part of any genre in precisely the same way as the rules of a game include the rules of the interaction of the partners.[8] But texts may, and frequently do, play several games – and thus several partners – at once.

The rest of my discussion will dwell on the level of genre, not of text. This is because I think there's a need for working over what we mean by this term.

Discussions of genre usually take the form of discussions of 'classes of text', or 'text types', and proceed on the basis of the assumption that a classification is constructed by a series of descriptions of similarity and difference. I shall start by doing just that, and go on to show how statements of similarity and difference require to be construed through the notion of ceremonial place. Tennis will recur, but only fleetingly. To discuss how a text plays its game(s) requires close readings – another genre.

'Like-statements'

'Like-statements' are statements which we use to classify things, either to establish the class, or to include something apparently different within it. Frequently they are strategies for sorting out what might count as salient properties, understanding something unfamiliar by asking whether it shares this or that feature with something familiar. To claim that items x, y, and z form a class is to make certain features salient above others, and to claim that these features go some way towards describing how each member functions, or is placed, in relation to others not sharing these features. In the description of genres, or of texts in terms of generic classifications, 'like-statements' look like this.

You could say that

an architect's plan is like a recipe;
and that a doctor's prescription is a recipe that can be made only by a qualified pharmacist.

You could also say that instructions for

making model aeroplanes;
reporting the results of a chemistry experiment;
preparing an article for publication in such and such a journal;
writing sonnets

are also like recipes. But do we get good sonnets and good science reports from instructions in this form? Recipes are a genre; but genres are not recipes.

'Not-statements'

Most theories of genre concentrate on 'like-statements'; most descriptions of individual texts in terms of generic generalizations concentrate on 'not-statements'. I want to propose a way of thinking about genre and genre theory that takes 'not-statements' as its starting-point.

Doors are like windows, but they are not windows.

It is important for us to know the difference between an architect's plan and a recipe, and it may be that this is best described in terms of social setting. Saying that we have something like the *same genre* turning up in different settings may be important for genre theory, in order to avoid the social-determinist position, which might claim:

1 that genres are specific to social (e.g. disciplinary or institutional) setting;
2 that social relations such as class and institutional hierarchies determine genre.

Such claims can be refuted by linguistic and discursive analysis of textual features.[9]

It is also important for us to know, and be able to describe, the difference between a doctor's prescription and a doctor's referral letter to another doctor. Being able to describe this difference is the business of genre theory, and knowing it in practice matters for getting on with the business of obtaining the right professional advice from the right 'person'. These two kinds of texts are strategies for doing two things.

1 dealing with a diseased and suffering body;
2 asserting the structural and functional relations that make a profession more than a collection of trained workers. This assertion needs to be made in order to make the profession work as such, and it also needs to be addressed to the patient, in order that she or he can make use of it as a profession. Not to do so is equivalent to misusing it, or using it incorrectly; it makes the system dysfunctional in respect of that case.

Let us suppose, then, that a 'medical consultation' is a ceremony, consisting of several genres: greeting, the eliciting of presenting symptoms, examination, decisions for treatment. Within each of these genres, different tactical moves are made by both players, and these moves can be described as speech acts – commands, requests, complaints, advice, reassurance, and so on – as well as the less formal acts that structure the relationship of doctor and patient. The question then arises whether there is any tactical leeway in the writing of prescriptions or referral letters. In the former case, it is minimized and regulated as much as possible, to guard against possible mistakes, but I am certain that if doctors would allow us to collect a corpus of their referral letters a considerable range of variation would be discernible. In particular, I would wager my professional integrity on the following hypothesis: that they have all sorts of ways of indicating to one another not only their medical judgements, but their assessments of the patient's supposed character, his or her way of handling suffering, and, specifically, his or her tactical manoeuvres in medical consultation. This last, of course, is unlikely to be described either in detail or as such: I suspect the patient's game-playing abilities are what provide the 'evidence' for assessments of character and personality.

We should also note that the fact that prescriptions are not typewritten, and the fact that doctors by and large give bad handwriting the status of a characteristic of their profession, are both liable to be described as tactics designed to preclude the patient from the position of addressee of this kind of text. However, the exclusiveness of the language used in prescriptions, though it may have this effect in a secondary way, is generic rather than tactical, since this language defines the professional relationship of doctor and pharmacist, and mediates their professional difference.

A medical consultation is not the same as a consultation with a lawyer: this is a difference of institution, but the ceremonial may be usefully described as similar. The consultation (patient to doctor, client to lawyer) is the ceremonial that situates the genre we call 'referral' in the one case and 'brief' in the other, but 'referral' and 'brief' may be similar, and when we say so we can make some sense of the variety of situations in which we find 'briefs'. A brief fulfils a certain function within a profession, mediating two functionally and hierarchically different places, such that one can request work from the other. It is frequently the case that the person to whom the brief is addressed is placed *by the brief* in the position of specialist, but this does not necessarily correspond with hierarchical superiority. A government, for example, briefs an expert, or a committee, from a position of uncontested authority, by contrast with the professional hierarchization which places an instructing solicitor 'below' the barrister he or she briefs. Briefs may also be addressed to and by colleagues who are formally or informally equal, such as requests to intervene in a debate or meeting 'from a different point of view'. A brief, in effect, mediates a highly complex network of different social placings, addressing a request where a simple hierarchy would address a command. Nevertheless, it does seem to be a rule that briefs cannot dictate from below to above; nor can they be addressed from a specialist to a place of authority. Like a command, a brief places boundaries or states parameters, defining the substantive form of the text that will be its uptake, and that text will respond by restating these, giving the brief as the site and source of its informing intentions. Tactics within the brief might include requests for advice, the provision of information describing the case in such a way as not to pre-empt specialist opinion, but so as to justify the choice of this, rather than another, specialist. In a medical system such as that which obtains in Australia, where all consultations of a specialist are mediated by a generalist, the manners of a referral letter include the request for advice and impose the obligation on the specialist to respond accordingly. That is, though the specialist may take over the effective treatment of the patient, he or she will inform the generalist of the diagnosis and decisions for treatment, thereby maintaining the fiction that he or she is acting on behalf of the generalist, and that the patient is the generalist's patient.

The manners of a referral letter and the response that it elicits are not those of a formal or informal discussion between the same two doctors about the same case. Such a discussion may occur before the writing of a referral letter, after the letter but before the patient's visit to the specialist, or at any time after this, during – or, indeed, following – treatment. What is different is certainly not the concepts deployed but the uptake expected in that place. Sometimes, indeed, the same information must be reproduced in a different place in order to take on a different function.

'Not-statements' are useful in precisely this sort of situation. The point of a not-statement is to make a distinction between two terms – kinds of texts –

which in other respects are described by a like-statement. Starting from the class of all texts, or discourse, the non-statement is the first move establishing a generic classification. Indeed, it is the first move establishing the very postulate of genre. Nevertheless, typical genre descriptions take the form: 'like ... but not ...' The 'like' part of the generic description establishes the domain of pertinent comparisons; the 'not' part establishes a boundary, not in the sense of a limitation, or a limit on possibilities, but in the sense of locating 'this kind' of text in a space, and *vis-à-vis* other kinds. The not-statement gives this kind a place among other places.

The strategy I use to describe the genre of a text is contrastive: it starts from a not-statement. This is by contrast with the recipe, which starts from the ingredients. To be effective, such negative descriptions rely on strategically chosen contrasting genres. For example, a recipe book is like (a) manuals, and other how-to books, and (b) menus. It is also unlike both in crucial respects, particularly because menus are not like manuals. The characteristic inclusion of handy hints, household advice, and personal anecdotes marks it off and allies it with still other genres.

'Not-statements' are not just made by genre theorists about texts: they are frequently made by texts themselves as a self-situating strategy. But they need not be in the explicit propositional form of a negative description. It is useful to note some examples of this explicit form before finding what might count as equivalents. For instance:

> This work is an essay in Peirce's epistemology, with about an equal emphasis on the 'epistemology' as on the 'Peirce's'. In other words our intention *has not been to write exclusively a piece of Peirce scholarship* – hence the reader will find no elaborate tying in of Peirce's epistemology to other portions of his thought, no great emphasis on the chronology of his thought, etc. Peirce scholarship is a painstaking business. His mind was labyrinthine, his terminology intricate, and his writings are, as he himself confessed, 'a snarl of twine'. This book *rather* is intended perhaps even primarily as an essay in epistemology, taking Peirce's as the focal point. The book *thus addresses a general philosophical audience and bears as much on the wider issue as on the man.*
>
> (William H. Davis, *Peirce's Epistemology*; my italics)[10]

Notice that the not-statement precedes the positive description, but that, even were they in the reverse sequence, the positive description would not be specific without the negative. Without the not-statement, the sentence 'This book ... is intended ... primarily as an essay in epistemology, taking Peirce's as the focal point' would tell us no more than the title: alone, the title sets up two possibilities – that this is an author study ('Peirce scholarship') and that this is a topic study ('epistemology'). When the not-statement is made, it distinguishes these as two genres of philosophic writing. The question of genre is tied to the question of audience, and thus to the question of expectations and predictions: a topic study is addressed to philosophers, whereas a book 'on Peirce' might well find that it had relatively few readers who defined themselves as philosophers, and relatively many from such fields as semiotics and literary theory. Peirce is in this respect something of a special case; yet were we to put, say, Kant in the place of the proper name of this title the specification would still hold, distinguishing, for instance, historians of ideas from philosophers in the technical sense.

Let us look at a second example:

> This book is nominally an abridgement of the *Concise Oxford Dictionary, but has in fact* cost its compilers more labour, partly because the larger book was found *not to be easily squeezable,* and partly owing to changes in method *un*connected with *mere* reduction in quantity. The one merit, however, that they feel entitled to claim for the C.O.D. has been preserved to the best of their power in the abridgement – that is, they have kept to the principle that *a dictionary is a book of diction, concerned primarily with words or phrases as such, and not,* except so far as is needed to ensure their right treatment in speech, *with the things those words and phrases stand for.* This principle, while it *absolves* the dictionary-maker *from encumbering his pages with encyclopaedic information, demands on the other hand that he should devote much more space than that so saved to the task of making clear the idiomatic usage of words.*
>
> (*The Pocket Oxford Dictionary*, preface to the first edition; my italics)[11]

It appears that the important not-statement is the one that contrasts the *Concise* with the *Pocket Oxford Dictionary*, but they are more 'like' than 'unlike' in that they share a not-statement that sets all dictionaries in contrast with another genre. The crucial contrast that constitutes the definition of a dictionary is that a dictionary is 'not an encyclopaedia'. This opposition, which plays out in a special way the 'words versus world' dichotomy, has needed to be made since the first encyclopaedias, dating from the eighteenth century, jostled for position in the space occupied by the much older, traditional genre which took on its conventional features in the age of humanism. The history of the encyclopaedia as genre is a most interesting question, which goes, I'm afraid, beyond my present brief. What I do wish to dwell on for a moment is the fact that 'a dictionary is not an encyclopaedia' seems to be a more important or urgent statement to make than, for example, 'a dictionary is not a grammar'. We might find the latter statement in treatises of linguistics. The former statement is found in those places where there is a possible confusion that arises as a result of a like-statement: the layout of dictionaries and encyclopaedias is very similar. They both have columns dividing their pages, and each column consists of an entry, having the *form of a word,* followed by explanatory information about that 'word'. Dictionaries, however, define these 'words' as 'diction' and 'usage'; encyclopaedias define them as the names of things. The convention whereby encyclopaedias illustrate their information with images – diagrams, photographs, maps, portraits, and the like – has as its function to demonstrate this distinction between the 'word' and what it names by showing the thing named in a form other than verbal. The convention whereby dictionaries illustrate their explanations of usage by *uses* (quotations) demonstrates their fundamental claim that the conventions of a language explain that language, that the rules of usage lie not outside the language but within it. When Ferdinand de Saussure[12] defined a language as 'something like a dictionary', he was relying on the generic conventions of dictionaries to make this analogy. When, furthermore, he defined a sign by its place within the rules of usage, *rather than* as the name of a thing, he was relying on the not-statement whereby dictionaries and encyclopaedias are contrasted, and he was saying that the generic conventions of dictionaries provide a better analogy than those of encyclopaedias for a linguist concerned with the problem of how a language determines meaning. (Since then, semioticians have done loads of interesting things with the (generalized) notion of the encyclopaedia. But all this, too, lies beyond my brief.)

Let me return briefly to my earlier statement that there is a difference between saying 'a dictionary is not an encyclopaedia' and 'a dictionary is not a grammar'. Each of these not-statements serves a particular purpose. The former, as I have said, plays out the 'words versus world' dichotomy; the latter serves to distinguish two different kinds of information that linguists provide in the descriptions of languages. Both, however, are statements about genre. This seems to suggest that a genre cannot be defined by a single not-statement, but rather that a generic definition ('definition' is, literally, 'the tracing of boundaries' rather than the discovery of an essence) arises as (or 'from') a series of contrasts which position 'this' kind in among other adjacent kinds of texts. Think, for instance, of the public-transport tickets available in your town or city. There may be:

single passes (for a one-way trip);
day passes (for travel between given hours on one day, using any number of vehicles and kinds of vehicles, in any direction);
weekly passes (similar to the above, but valid over a longer period);
monthly passes (ditto).

The differences between the tickets giving you these rights will be marked in a variety of ways: they may be colour-coded, and a difference may be made between those that must last (printed on card) and those that *must not* last (printed on flimsy paper). Single fares will be identified by the amount paid, but passes for longer periods will be identified with dates and times. They may also be personalized. It is useful to recall from this example that, although we might be inclined to believe that the genre is marked inherently on each kind of ticket, those markings only work because they are correlated with *places in a system of contrasts*. To rely on the inherent features of each is the 'recipe theory of genre'; to take into consideration the system of contrasts is the alternative that I am proposing.

Here is a third example of a not-statement by a text:

What you will be reading here are the results of my research. *They are not intended as a biography* in the usual sense, *but as a kind of casebook*, told in the words of those who were closest to the individual at the time.
(Martin Buzacott, *Charivari*; my italics)[13]

Think about who writes casebooks, and for what purposes. Buzacott's claim (for his fiction, note!) is not only that it is 'true'. It uses the documentary mode to contest the coherent narrative form that makes the subject of a biography a hero. The subject of this study is a 'case', appearing in 'documents' independent of the storytelling proclivities of a narrator.

A fourth example is as follows:

> This form is *not* to be completed by people who propose only a visit to Australia or a period of temporary *rather than* permanent settlement.
>   *Separate forms* are available for these purposes.
> (Department of Immigration and Ethnic Affairs application for entry for settlement; my italics)[14]

The not-statements in this text distinguish forms for prospective immigrants from forms for tourist visas and temporary-settlement visas. This distinction is crucial for the work of the Immigration Department, but it may be far less crucial for a theorist of discourse whose brief is, for instance, to describe the genres in use in Australian government offices, and who might be tempted to group all 'forms' together. Questions of layout, printing, kinds of purpose, and the function of spaces on the form are common to all forms. We 'know' a form when we see one, and, although an immigration form might ask for a certain amount of information that you would also find, for instance, in a curriculum vitae, nevertheless we know the difference between these two genres. On the other hand, having made the statement I have just made, it occurs to me that it may be useful to group together c.v.s and forms, and to say that the crucial difference between them is in the social settings in which they function. Both work to identify a person in a 'liminal' situation, attempting to pass from one space into another, and both present the information that might be necessary for that passage to be authorized. However, here I am discussing the curriculum vitae as if it were co-extensive with a job application, whereas in fact it is only a part of it; in isolation, a curriculum vitae is more like a biography whose events are listed rather than narrated. Job applications and visa applications are by and large the same ceremonial, used in different institutions.

This discussion illustrates an observation I made earlier – that different classificatory statements make different features salient. It also demonstrates that different like-statements and different not-statements are used for different purposes. This suggests that 'genre' is not absolute (let alone 'primitive', as some linguistic uses of the term need it to be); it is pragmatic. This does not mean, however, that it is merely whimsical, or subjective. It means that

1 generic descriptions are a genre;
2 this genre turns up as a game in a variety of social settings:
   filing systems;
   library classification systems;
   publishing and bookselling;
   institutional administration;

the construction of school syllabuses;
any theoretical activity designed to describe the pragmatics of discourse;
and so on.

It also has a great deal to do with how we separate the learned disciplines from one another.

I have suggested above that not-statements can be made in a variety of ways and are not restricted to explicit negative descriptions. Two of my examples illustrate this point. The transport tickets make their not-statements by means of the variety of contrastive codings that I have sketched out. Forms make not-statements with black lines, and code these lines as 'heavy' or 'light' in order to group bits of information and separate them off from other groups. Just as dictionaries and encyclopaedias use two kinds of typeface to distinguish 'word' and 'explanation' within the entry, and paragraphing and columns to distinguish entries, so do other kinds of printed objects adopt these sorts of typographical techniques as ways of saying 'not that, but this'. Columns do not, but boxes do, distinguish articles in a newspaper or magazine, and conventions of paging as well as boxing organize such objects into ordered collections of genres. The system of titles that override headlines makes these classifications explicit where this is necessary. The same news item may occur twice in the same issue of the same newspaper, working to 'mean something different' depending on the genre with which it is grouped. Such things as an event in the business community may count as 'news' on page 1 or 2, and be repeated as useful information for investors in the Business Pages. The death of a famous person may count as news, and then be repeated, for instance as an obituary, somewhere else (some papers have quasi-permanent obituary columns). If the famous person is a woman, the obituary may be printed on the Women's Pages (which are generically distinguished in most Australian newspapers), or these same pages may carry a general article about the woman and her work, using the death as pretext and occasion. Women's Pages in newspapers function to make the statement 'Women count as news, too'; which is precisely a way of saying that we don't – or, at least, that it's not the same kind of news!

It may be argued that such considerations on newspaper and magazine layout are too mechanically formal to count as genuine genre descriptions. I wish to argue the contrary, but, of course, the lines and squares do not in and of themselves count as generic descriptions. They are the not-statements, which are tied to the like-statements. They work to say 'this is like news' and also 'this is like other articles of interest to the girls'. Then we need to find out what is implied by such a grouping. 'News' makes the death of Simone de Beauvoir 'like' any news item involving an internationally famous person; but the locating of an article about her life and work on the Women's Pages makes the *salient feature* the fact that she was a woman. The not-statement suggests that classifying might always be *re*classifying, that it is useful to think of it as an act, and a strategy; it also suggests that the 'place' of the text in some sense *precedes* the features that we take to be characteristic of it.

The metaphor of 'place'

The metaphor of place is not a mere convenience in genre theory. Its tactical usefulness goes back for centuries, and is one of the generic markers of the treatises on 'Poetics' following the authorial example set by Aristotle. Indeed, it may well be the case that the metaphor of place is more than a tactic; there are good reasons for thinking that it is actually germane to the problem of making classifications in general, and generic classifications in particular. It may not, then, be an accident that we so often use diagrams to represent taxonomical and other classificatory forms, that we talk about 'borderline cases' when we are not sure whether something fits in this, or another, class, or that when we describe the genres of television and radio we use the notion of the 'time slot'. I shall return to this last non-accident shortly.

PLACE AND SETTING

The most widespread traditional distinction between genres is the distinction between the 'high' and the 'low' genres of literature, and it is by this means that 'tragedy' is opposed to 'comedy', and 'epic' to chronicles. The ode, likewise, is opposed to personal lyric poetry as high is to low. The high forms can be 'mocked' by imitating them, writing about typically 'low' subjects in the forms appropriate for the grand and the glorious. Pope's *The Rape of the Lock* and Byron's *Don Juan* are obvious examples. But such allusions to the high by the low are not only for the purposes of mockery: the title Balzac chose for his vast collection of novels set in the urban inferno of early nineteenth-century Paris was *La Comédie humaine*. This title alludes most obviously to Dante's *Divine Comedy*; where the latter is an epic journey through the divine scheme of things, Balzac's work is concerned with the failure of any 'scheme' – let alone divine – to provide rational bases for a society formed, or deformed, by early capitalism in the aftermath of the French Revolution, or to provide a rational account of such a world. But Balzac's title also makes us dwell on the notion of 'comedy': there is no sense in which the squalor and corruption he describes are comic, although his characters are in the best tradition of the caricatural types of satire. Rather, 'comedy' has come to mean in nineteenth-century France the whole institution of the theatre: this is, Balzac might be telling us, *like* the theatre, in that the world is governed by the laws of disguise and dissimulation, peopled and furnished by simulations, fakes, forgeries, and pseudonyms.[15] These are the laws of lawlessness. Yet the conventions of realist writing force us towards the other half of the generic description: like the theatre, this is not the theatre. This is outside the theatre – *la comédie française*, perhaps? – and it is the Real. The generic description is at issue in Balzac in the most precise way: the novel is not a play, and, if everything followed this rule, the world would continue to make sense. But if the Real is like the Theatre, such that spectators are caught up as participants in the fabrication and perpetuation of an illusory reality which they can no longer distinguish as illusory, then the distinction between true and false, and the moral distinctions that it grounds, can no longer be made. Now comedy, traditionally, is the genre that disturbs the distinctions between high and low that tragedy relies on and reaffirms.

'High' and 'low' – the possibility of distinguishing one from the other, the meaning each derives from its opposition with the other – also traditionally refer to the social and topographical settings characteristic of certain genres. The 'noble' forms are set among kings and princes, heroes and divinities; tragedy can only happen to the great, as a spectacle for lesser mortals. Epic has the choice of legendary, foundationalist myth, and the founding wars of nations; its scale is vast, and its characters drawn in line with their vocation, which is to guide and govern the destiny of humankind. In the nineteenth century, the high form is no doubt grand opera, set against novels of urban realism, and enacting the conflicts of love and political intrigue among the mighty. True to the calling of the high forms, Wagner exhibits their law in his choice of mythical subjects and divine destinies. But this law is confirmed with equal force by its violation: the courtesan rather than the courtier (*La Traviata, Madama Butterfly*); the simple folk instead of the aristocracy (*Peter Grimes, Porgy and Bess*); the poor and the marginal (*La Bohème*). Yet in each case the genre of the opera has the effect of 'elevating' its subject to stand, as a king or his daughter might do, as the site of the victory of the 'slings and arrows of outrageous fortune'. That *La Bohème* does this in the case of artists; that *Peter Grimes* and *Porgy and Bess* do it for fisherfolk at odds with the ungovernable forces of nature; and that *La Traviata* allows illness to do the bidding of the rich and powerful, confirming the essential nobility of the abandoned courtesan, only confirm that the Subject of the high forms is Destiny played out in exceptional individuals. How different a thing is dying, in the *Three Lives* of Gertrude Stein.[16]

It is because the metaphor of the high forms can be taken so literally in terms of class and power that those forms that contest their validity for a 'modern' world so often produce it in its stock form – the metaphor of the mountain peak. Set against this are flat lands, urban landscapes, hovels, villages. While the slopes or the peaks of a mountain are the typical setting for the encounter of gods and men, in these other places men are left largely to their own devices. Yet, frequently, the opposition itself turns up to comment on or to transform its classical use. Balzac's use of the boarding-house hierarchy (the poorer you are, the higher you go) neatly reverses the figure. Eco's abbey conforms to it in its most classical form, though things get rather mixed up in the kitchen.[17] In *The Ponder Heart* Eudora Welty opposes the 'high house' to the hotel in the township of Clay; it is in the latter – and ultimately in the courthouse – that the stories of the high house are told. Each of these places is associated with a different kind of storytelling. It is at table in the hotel that Uncle Daniel holds his audience spellbound, and it is here too that the end of the novel is marked by the disappearance of the audience and the difficulty of getting Uncle Daniel to *come down* from his room. It is also at the hotel that the narrator captivates

– or is it captures? – her solitary listener, to tell the tale of these other tellings. But it is in the high house that she finds Bonny Dee's reading matter:

> I'm a great reader that never has time to read.
>
> Little old Bonnie Dee had six years of *True Love Story* and six years of *Movie Mirror* stacked up on the sewing machine . . . and the hatrack in the hall, and down behind the pillows on the sofa. She must have read her heart out. Or at least she'd cut out all the coupons with her scissors. I saw by the holes she'd left where she'd sent off for all kinds of things – you know, wherever they showed the postman smiling in the ad. I figures she must have got back, some time or other, twenty-four samples of world-famous perfumes; and a free booklet on how to speak and write masterly English . . .; and a free piano lesson to prove you can amaze your friends; and a set of Balzac to examine ten days free of charge, but she must have decided against it – I looked everywhere. So there were holes in the stories all the way through, but they wouldn't have lasted me long anyway. I read *The House of the Thousand Candles* for the thousandth time; and the rest of the time I cleaned the house.[18]

In the context of this opposition, the settings of novels and plays are not mere décor; they are generic markers, understood as situating their texts in a map of possible places. Such things as factories, family homes, houses away from town versus houses in town, etc., count as conventions for such purposes in just the same way as a pastoral setting does for 'pastoral' and the streets of a city for graffiti. But these conventions do not act alone. The example of graffiti can point us in another direction: 'place' is no mere metaphor. Where a text occurs is germane to its generic function, because who it is addressed to is governed by material factors such as this. A society is, in this sense, a system of quite literal places, and the setting of a text may be read as a symbolic representation of the work the text does to find a place in which to speak and an audience on which to act. In this connection, it is worth recalling that the novel inaugurates an essentially private mode of reading: its knowledge of the human heart is quite precisely its way of speaking to it of its contents. Social-realist writing takes its reader to the window, contesting the code of the sentimental wherein a personal space is constructed as inward. Balzac (again!) speaks to his leisured bourgeois reader, telling her to use his book to reach beyond the world to which she has been consigned.[19] The typical spaces of the novel are governed not by the opposition of the high and the low, but by that essentially horizontal axis of the inner and the outer that has at one extreme the private spaces of personal sentiment, and at the other the city (Dickens), a country (Gordimer, Rushdie), a world (Lessing). Domestic spaces – hotels, apartment blocks, family homes – are the necessary mediators of this axis.[20]

PLACE AND TIME

All generic descriptions rely on a more or less explicit 'filing system', and it is said that the earliest attempts to formalize genre theory arose from the need to rationalize the classifications and systems of location of the collections in the great libraries of the ancient world. It is clear in this example that 'place' must be taken quite literally, and the same is true of newspaper layout. Taking the index, always to be found on one of the outside pages of a newspaper, certain rules concerning the location of given kinds of items can be discerned. This is not to say that the television programmes and meteorology reports will always be found on page 10; rather, they will never be found on the first page. Similarly, it is not helpful to think of library locations as corresponding to particular shelves in particular rows; rather, PN books come before PQ books, and after B books. This suggests that the notion of place that we need in order to discuss such questions is relational rather than absolute, and that such systems have a time or a sequence built into them, such that they impose a pattern of use which determines what counts as first and last, before and following, front and back. The rules for the use of the system are rules for mapping together actual spaces, such as library buildings, with systemic places, such as the Library of Congress classification. They are set out in indexes, guides to classifications and locations, and tables of contents, and these are necessarily sequential. Television and radio programmes do the same sort of thing with actual times.

Another sense in which the notion of place must be taken quite literally in the description of genre is this: some kinds of texts occur necessarily, or always, in kinds of places, between participants defined by their social roles. The briefs and referral letters I mentioned earlier are a case in point; so would be the rulings of an administrative tribunal or a judge. Office memoranda, lectures, board meetings, and a million other examples, must be defined in this way, and it is clear that what gets said, and the kinds of interlocutory relationships that are produced, are largely determined by this notion of place. I might tell a story about how someone jostled me in a queue, or how someone pulled rank to be promoted ahead of me, or seen out of turn at the doctor's. If I tell this story to my neighbour over a drink, it is a story about the other person, or about social injustice; but, if I tell the same story to my psychiatrist, it is a story about me, my lack of personal confidence, and my failure to self-assert. John Berger may give his essay about Paris[21] to his psychoanalyst, who will find that it deploys a series of figures of intimacy. 'Where's the towel, Maman?' becomes in this rendition the moment where the assertion that 'this is my home, my birthplace, the scene of my intimate selfhood' is identified as the point of the telling. But in a class on the semiotics of iconicity and the conventions of so-called likenesses this reading is 'out of place'.[22]

This expression leads me to suggest that when we are talking about genre, and ceremonials, it may be useful to talk about 'the manners of a text'. If the rhetorical rules of a genre are thought of as an etiquette, rather than as fixed laws, it is easier for us to think of them as being to do with how people get on with one another. In some cases, etiquette is best thought of as rules appropriate to a pre-existing situation, but this is far less often the case than we might suppose. Manners are instrumental in organizing and determining role-relations, and thus in forming settings. They 'make' the person, in more senses than one. Etiquette may be written as an immutable code, and expressed in the form of dogmatic deontics; when it is, we tend to find it ridiculous and out of date. But this does not mean that we don't observe an etiquette appropriate to whatever occasion, and social groups continually renegotiate the forms of acceptable behaviour in relation to an implicit or explicit criterion of appropriateness. We take for granted that such rules are pretty arbitrary, and we may be more comfortable with the fiction that our rules are not real rules, and need not be spoken. But even this fiction is 'good manners' in a group that thinks of itself as unregulated by anything but spontaneity and fellow feeling. Such rules, like the rules of a genre or of a ceremony, are there to 'make things work'. Nevertheless, manners are never a matter of simple conformity with a normative model. They can be used for the purposes of an interaction, not just followed; they are good or bad shots, productive or not of situations requiring inventive uptakes.

The identification of time slots in television programming is a particularly interesting case, which shows, among other things, that the 'place' precedes the 'internal' features of a given genre. The identification of kinds of audiences by the times of the evening at which they might watch the box is also a factor in the determination of those audiences: 'children's', 'family viewing', 'late night', and so on, are slots in rather the same way as in a printed form which organizes bits of information into different places on a sheet of paper, and thereby creates groupings and ways of relating those bits of information. They may even create, or determine, that information. Given the economics of TV programming, it is an important fact about televisual genres that they are written for, produced for, and bought for slots, and not the other way around. But these slots are not just empty spaces; they are spaces in a relational system that is organized around key points – before and after the early and mid-evening news, to take the most obvious example (this is called 'the hook') – which have the function of marking boundaries, and thus making the not-statements that produce the major differentiations.[23] It is an interesting fact that it is the news programmes that have this crucial function: this is the genre that makes explicit the major generic distinction in Australian television – the differentiation of 'information' from 'entertainment' – and at the same time shows the extent to which the patterns of television programming are derivative of the patterns of arrangements of texts that make up newspapers and magazines.

A recent survey of television violence is of some interest here. It has long been an assumption of most work in the sociology of television that there is 'more violence' in the 'late night' slot than in the 'family viewing' or 'children's' slots, but, when explicit criteria for the identification of violence were used, this was shown not be be the case. There is a great deal more violence in, for instance, cartoons than in the genres where we might expect to find it – police series, thrillers, horror movies, and the like. What seems to be at issue here is that it doesn't count as violence in sports programmes, cartoons, and soap operas. What counts as television violence for the sociologist is what counts as socially dangerous. It is 'not dangerous' to show a crocodile mauling a body; not dangerous to show a punch-up on a football field; not dangerous to show a character zapping another beyond all recognition in a cartoon. This is because what counts as violence for the viewer is governed – 'made intelligible' – by generic criteria. It is these that rationalize it and make it acceptable. To be the viewer of a cartoon is to know the difference between fantasy and the real; to be the viewer of a sports programme is to be on a side; to be the viewer of the news is to do your duty, knowing what's going on in the world, however nasty it might be. The moral dimension of 'realism' has its full force here. It may well be that the violent content in such programmes is more worrying on some criteria than the conventional struggle of marginal characters with each other and the forces of law and order, but the point is not, for the moment, there. The 'content' of victors and victims is the same; it just works differently, has a different status, and thus means something different, depending (a) on its relation with other generic conventions, and (b) on its slot and the production of viewing habits in a type-audience. This is the same point as that made in speech-act theory, according to which 'the same propositional content' functions differently, and thus means something different, according to its performative setting. Meaning is not content; it is place and function.

PLACE AND FUNCTION

Let me retrieve my problem of games and ceremonials. In, for example, court proceedings, the important stages or phases of the event can be said to be places (or times) marked out and occupied by different kinds of texts. The clerk of the court reads what counts as the title of the hearing, the proper names in a conventional order that shows which is defendant and which prosecution. There is the choice and swearing in of the members of the jury, where appropriate, and the judge's instructions to them; the opening addresses of the counsel; calling of witnesses and cross-examination; addresses to the jury; the jury's deliberations; their recall and pronounce-ment; the judge's address and passing of sentence. Each of these moments is a genre, though it may be occupied by several texts, and each of the texts will deploy a range of tactics. It is, of course, quite possible to isolate, say, all the texts pronounced by the prosecution counsel, or the judge, or a witness, and there are certain purposes – for instance, for the jury's deliberations – which make this a useful thing to do. Anybody studying the career or personality of one of these participants would likewise need to make this set of choices, rather than the choices governed strictly by generic criteria. Yet it would be misleading to overlook the generic place of the texts, even in such a study, for to do so would be to neglect the question of strategy – what is said, not said, and how represented – for the particular purposes dictated by a given 'place' in the proceedings. To understand the rules of the genre is to know when and where it is appropriate to do and say certain things, and to know that to do and say them at inappropriate places and times is to run the risk of having them ruled out. To use these rules with skill is to apply questions of strategy to decisions of timing and the tactical plan of the rhetoric.

The same sorts of considerations bear on the decision to use, for instance, the place of a speech at a graduation ceremony to make a statement about the funding of graduate study, or an after-dinner speech to pull the rug from under a beset and beleaguered politician. All sorts of things may be said on such occasions; the genre of the after-dinner speech is not set by its inherent features so much as by the range of uses to which this place can be put. Nevertheless, it must be stressed that 'place' in this sense is not empty, neutral, or uninformed. Just as with the television audiences, the roles of the two interlocutory participants, their predictions, and the kind of behaviour that is appropriate to them are set by the occasion. These may indeed determine features inherent to the modes of address, and a text can be fruitfully studied for the way in which it constructs its audience positions. These may well be genre-specific, but a lot of work remains to be done before we find the most useful ways of describing them. What we can say, however, is that it is place, in the complex of meanings I have attempted to sketch out for this term, that determines the reading of linguistic or other formal features. It is most unlikely, however, that any linguistic feature taken in isolation could be held to be characteristic of a genre; rather, what we might expect is that combinations of features might count as the conventional markers of a genre. It is quite another question whether such combinations of features count as *constitutive* of a genre in the same way that the use of performative verbs in the first-person, present-tense indicative mood constitutes the typical case of many speech acts. My argument leads me to suggest that it is place, rather, that constitutes genre, and that the functions and roles entailed by place determine the interlocutory structure of a genre. Conversely, if one of the tasks of a text is to mark itself generically in relation to others in order to get its partners to play ball in the appropriate manner, this can be said to constitute at least some of the parameters of its place.

PLACE AND FRAMING

The notion that our texts arise within ceremonials, and that their form is determined by their ceremonial place and function, can be restated to say that the ceremonial frames a time and space, setting it apart from others, and marking its specificity. The distinction I made earlier, between 'a game' and 'the playing of that game', can also be made between a piece of music and its performance, and between a play and its performance. The performance in either case is not restricted to the players: it includes the constitution of the audience, their assembly in a particular time and place, and the rituals whereby that assembly marks the audience *as* audience, rather than as a collection of discrete units, setting them in position to make the playing possible. Reading a book, attending and giving lectures, dinner conversations, filling in forms, interviews – and a host of others – are all ceremonial frames and/or the genres that occur within them. On this view, it is not stretching the point to argue that the publishing conventions that make books what they are – with covers, titles, bibliographical and cataloguing information, title pages, tables of contents, acknowledgements, prefaces by series editors, footnotes, indexes, glossaries, etc. – are notational frames for the ceremonies of reading. The variety of liminal and closing texts, their arrangement, and their formal features, have a great deal to do with the business of setting the genre of the text they enclose. A book is a material space, like an office or a classroom. Like books, the material arrangement of the space in which a text occurs has a bearing on the sense of that text and has a lot to do, necessarily, with the briefs we give the architects of the institutional, industrial, commercial, and domestic spaces that design our signs. A discussion between two executives, one slightly superior in the company hierarchy to the other, will work differently, depending on whether the piece of furniture between them is a desk or a lunch table, and depending on whether the desk is the superior's or his subordinate's. The piece of furniture together with other 'props' define a space and the ceremonial appropriate to it. It may well be that the participants might try to have 'the same' discussion in both places, but the choice of one or another ceremonial alters the conditions of speech and understanding. We might be inclined to say that the choice of lunch for such business conversations is 'more relaxed', or a way of getting away from the formal rituals of the office with its hierarchies; but I think this is misleading. We never leave the space of rituals for a space of non-rituals; we choose one ritual instead of another.

It is clear in this example that the notion of 'genre' and that of 'ceremonial' are effectively co-extensive; but it is equally clear in the example of the court proceedings that this is not the case. Neither would it be useful to make 'genre' and 'ceremonial' coincide when talking about the theatre, or about music. A sonata has formal properties which make it recognizable as a sonata in the printed score, differentiating it crucially from a concerto, in much the same way as the latter is differentiated from a symphony. Criteria such as solo versus orchestral playing, the relation of soloist to the orchestra (outside the orchestra, or within it), as well as the formal harmonic properties associated with instrumental arrangements such as these, are important here. Some musical genres have effectively lapsed with the virtual disappearance of live home entertainment, and in this case, too, it is important to specify both the generic and the ceremonial criteria. Some genres, on the other hand, subsist in different ceremonials from the ones in which they conventionally arose. In such cases, they take with them the signs of the lost ceremony, connoting that ceremony and the social relations it governs. For all these reasons, the problem of the formal properties of a genre will not go away.

In the history of genre theory, it is a remarkable fact that we have not, by and large, felt the need to theorize or otherwise make explicit the features of those genres which are so thoroughly specified by their ceremonial places that they seem self-evident. With the recent interest shown by the linguists of discourse in these questions, this is changing. Discovering the implicit rules for the self-evident is the very project of the linguist and the sociologist. But traditional genre theory rarely asked what the constitutive form of a prayer or a sermon was,[24] and, although certain questions about the rhetoric of preaching, pleading, and other forms of public speaking were indeed the stock-in-trade of the treatises of oratory, these were broached as questions of etiquette and of tactics, as if the question of generic specificity was unproblematical. It seems that genre theory has only been concerned to differentiate those genres that can occupy the same or very similar places. So we have worried about the differences among the genres of the theatre, but not about the difference between novels and plays. Within the history of philosophy, and library cataloguing, we had to worry about the difference between psychology and the philosophy of mind, placing considerable distance between them to signify that difference. And since the Renaissance we have come to worry about the generic specificity of what we call 'poetry', because the ceremonials defining the place of lyric verse (e.g. accompanied recitation) have been lost. Verse itself has been said to be not constitutive of poetry, and, following the loss of a musical setting, the typesetting conventions have also been disturbed: poetry has 'broken bounds' as it has come to be read under material and ceremonial conditions very similar to those appropriate to the reading of prose fiction. The continual debate about 'prose' and 'poetry' is a debate about a contested boundary; but it is also the play for generic specificity *within the same space*. My very strong suspicion is that we can generalize from this case: the question of the constitutive status of formal features arises when, and only when, there is more than one game possible in a single ceremonial setting.

It is usual to discuss the formal properties of a genre by listing them: comedy has *a*, *b*, and *c*; tragedy has *x*, *y*, and *z*. Yet it seems to me that what we do with genres is not to know them inherently but to know – 'tell', or enact – the differences *between them*. Thus we might say, about the tragedies and comedies of Shakespeare, that their settings are different (at court or in a noble castle, site of political power, versus in a forest, garden, or on the shores of an unknown country); that they are identified by the presence or absence of war; that they use different dictions (verse and prose are the marks of noble and ordinary speech respectively); that they differ in the domains of their typical subjects (the government of men, or human feelings and failings). Though both thematize the theatre itself, as the art of illusion, the modes of fiction that perform this function in the tragedies are lying, trickery, clandestine acts, whereas those whereby the problematics of fiction are explored in the comedies are disguise – anything from yellow stockings and cross-gartering to travesty – practical jokes, dreams, elaborate metaphors. These are formal conventions, but I would contest that they are 'inherent'. In each case, they play out the set of oppositions whereby tragedy and comedy are understood in relation to one another, and it is the opposition that constitutes the pair. Now exactly that which frames the illusion as a theatrical fiction without ultimate consequences in reality – that which sets it outside what counts as reality – is the typical comic setting outside the walls, in exile, in an unspecified or mythical geography. By contrast, that which invests the theme of illusion with moral and tragic consequences is a setting which marks out a space which has no outside, and which therefore works to stand for a society or a nation. (Macbeth cannot be banished, but must be killed within and by the space he has disrupted; and Lear's wanderings fail to take him effectively outside the space of his own demise.) That is to say that something that can be seen as a 'feature of' a genre is equally well seen as a framing mechanism whereby its status *vis-à-vis* other genres, its ceremonial place, and the mode of so-called reading are specified. Diction, setting, subject domains, and the rituals of conflict are not usefully described as distinct features. It is the system of their relations that frames, *and thus situates*, a text as genre.

This does not mean, of course, that the formal properties of a genre cannot travel, and it is now commonplace among genre theorists concerned primarily with literature that texts plunder the features of a variety of genres. Even the forms that are apparently most fixed – the sonnet, detective fiction – give up or borrow properties from a wide variety of other genres. Indeed, writing to a genre is itself a game, which can be played with more or less brinkmanship or bravado. Breaking the rules is, paradoxically, a way of asserting generic place. Since Horace, the real topic of literary theory has been the mixing of genres, and it is common, for example, to discuss Shakespeare's history plays as mixing the generic features of tragedy with those of comedy. A history play is 'like but not' a tragedy, since it is concerned with human destiny and treats of moral politics at the site of power. It is also 'like but not' a comedy, since its real subject can be said to be human failings rather than the edicts of destiny. Yet this is manifestly not an adequate account. The histories do not simply fall between the polar opposites of tragedy and comedy; using some of the features of each, they are also, crucially, not chronicles. Let us consider, briefly, an example.

To all intents and purposes, *Richard III* has all the features of, and therefore is, a tragedy, and its status as a history play is simply contingent on its characters' not being fictional, but chronicled elsewhere in the history of the English monarchy. Yet its framing as history is not so much contingent as crucial to its appropriate uptake. It matters to the moral purport of this play that it be understood as not mythical. Indeed, though there are ghosts, they are the ghosts of bad and good conscience, and there are no witches, prophecies, or other signs of an ineluctable destiny. This is a play about the interplay of self-interest and jealousy, where the evil king is neither the hero with a flaw nor the pawn of a greater power, but the synecdochal representative of the whole pattern of conflict, spite, and fawning in which he emerges. That it is like, but not, a tragedy, is the statement that corresponds to the formation of an appropriate posture for reading the play. The statement about what it is is contingent on this primary contrast. This statement – that it is a history play – is made both by the setting of some scenes in London and the *realpolitik* negotiations with the Lord Mayor, and, more pointedly, by the Prince of Wales, the next victim of that history:

PRINCE. I do not like the Tower, of any place.
    Did Julius Caesar build that place, my lord?
BUCK. He did, my gracious lord, begin that place,
    Which since, succeeding ages have re-edified.

PRINCE. Is it upon record, or else reported
    Successively from age to age, he built it?
BUCK. Upon record, my gracious lord.
PRINCE. But say, my lord, it were not register'd,
    Methinks the truth should live from age to age,
    As 'twere retail'd to all posterity,
    Even to the general all-ending day.

(Richard III, III. i)

Like a chronicle, this is not a chronicle; for it is also like a tragedy, and, though it is like a tragedy, yet its action is strangely close, set where the acting itself takes place, addressed to an audience whose ties to that time and place are not broken by the ceremonial of the theatre, but posited by it.

The notion of a ceremonial is particularly apt for those kinds of texts which depend upon time for their crucial medium. It is less obviously appropriate for those texts that are more precisely governed by space than by time. Yet the notion of framing takes over here in all its non-metaphorical force: the framing and placing of paintings and photographs, the pedestals of sculpture and its location inside and outside buildings or overlooking, or being overlooked by, a landscape – these are mechanisms that not only set such objects apart from their surroundings, but also locate them in relations of adjacency, similarity, and contrast with other objects and other texts. The framing of a photograph is not only the white surround; it is also crucially the compositional, lighting, and focus techniques that situate the object of the photograph in the image. The notion of framing can also be extended to include the place where photographs are put to be viewed and used, and the institutional settings in which they are made. To call all these things 'framing devices' may obscure their specificities. Yet what is important is the fact that the notion of place has all these dimensions, that place is entailed in genre – in the spatial genres most precisely – and that 'framing' is not usefully restricted to that which lies outside a text, but strategically includes those things which the text itself does to situate itself in relation to its social, formal, and material surroundings.[25]

A 'frame', or a boundary, is the enabling condition for a not-statement. One last example, this time from architecture, is borrowed from the work of John Macarthur.[26] If 'cottage' is the name of a genre, is't thinking makes it so? If we were to study all the buildings that were called cottages in eighteenth-century England, we would find that they include domestic dwellings, ranging from the most modest to something approaching a mansion, made of a number of materials, and of astonishing stylistic heterogeneity. This is a marvellous example for the anti-genre people. The 'pattern books' too (in which architects and philanthropists published designs for cottages), though apparently on the 'recipe' principle, demonstrate the full range of style and social status. Yet this is the beginning of an analysis of the problem: the cottage is a genre (like the almost contemporaneous novel) that is supposed to blend the high and the low. It does so, however, by lying between them, defined by two not-statements: it is neither hovel nor mansion. Like the literary pastoral, cottages are the place of retirement from 'the world', whether the world be the City and Society, or whether it be the fields of agricultural labour. Their exact situation in relation to other key sites in the estate is a significant issue, serving to distinguish between cottages that are sites for the pastoral dream, and objects and emblems in it. A cottager's cottage (as distinct from a gentleman's cottage – for there are, of course, two sub-genres) is economically defined as self-sufficient, since it has room for one cow and a kitchen garden, and as not autonomous, since it is leasehold, not freehold, and the lease of the cottage is tied to faithful labour for the freeholder. The building and design of cottagers' cottages is, moreover, governed by very precise social-policy considerations, defining the economic and labour relations between agricultural labourers, the estates, and contingently the parishes, on the one hand, and, on the other, a family unit not only bounded, as it were, on the outside, but determined by and determining gender relations and moral duties, on the inside.

Macarthur's argument is designed to show, among other things, that the genre of the cottage is identified by two non-coincident sets of frames: the mythical frame, determined in large measure by the goals of 'architecture proper', which marks out an ideal space to be occupied by such buildings, denying the class relations which are by that very denial asserted; and the class and economic frames. The latter frames specify the two sub-genres, and thus specify gentlemen's cottages as a pastoral dream, marked by signs of cottageness, but neither occupying a (topographical or social) space nor marking out spaces within it that in any way resemble the cottage as it is built to perform the social function, or to enact the moral political imperatives of the philanthropic programmes. Gentlemen's cottages are not cottagers' cottages, though they stand for the nostalgic dream of the simple life; and cottagers' cottages are emphatically not gentlemen's cottages. Everything about the design, location, and construction of these buildings conspires to make these statements.

IV

Reflections for an ending

* When all's said and done – though, as Peirce said, it never is – interpretation is classification is semiosis, and it is infinite.
* The question of genre is always the question of reading: the class to which a text is assigned is mutually entailed with the uptake of that text. To dwell on genre is thus to dwell on that question, doubly.
* What taxonomies are available to take up our texts? Many, and they do not agree. To read 'genre' is to read conflict.
* The metageneric is generic to genre. Thus genre is heterogeneous with itself.[27]

* The assignation of a text to a genre is already its reading: let us read that assignation and its machinery. This is the genre of genre theory.

THE THEORY OF GENRE

One of my more deliberate provocations has been to take filing systems – catalogues, programme schedules, and the like – as systems of genres. In itself, this is no big deal. But one of its implications is to bring Aristotle's *Poetics* into the same series. Likewise the series includes the classifications implied by the like- and not-statements whereby a text annexes generic predicates, placing itself alongside and in contrast with a field of others. The intention of suggesting this series is in the first instance to demystify the business of generic taxonomies. They are the administration of reading. But let us not be misled. It may well be that the logic of all classifications rests on the not-statement; and it may well also be that all classifications are in this crucial particular and its consequences similar. But there are *kinds* of classification. It would be illusory to suppose that they can be collapsed into one another, or that the metageneric descriptions they severally provide necessarily converge to reveal the nature of any genre. Indeed, I think the opposite is the case. If what we want is a general theory of genre, we might expect one of its axioms to be that metageneric pronouncements made in these places serve different purposes. As such, they will neither correlate nor synthesize. Classifications are themselves a rhetoric – a mode of address and the construction of an audience. Their heterogeneity is as much the business of a semiotics of genre as are the multiplicity and variety of the genres they purport to account for.

The so-called 'problem' of genre has always emerged in the failure of generic labels fully to describe their objects, the capacity of texts to lend themselves to a variety of descriptions, the difficulty of specifying the properties of any genres. But this is a problem only if the telos of the classification is truth. This is clearly not the case. The criterion of a good filing system is convenience, or ease of access: a misfiled document cannot be used, a miscatalogued book is read only with difficulty, rendered impertinent by its foreign frame.[28] On the other hand, a document filed in a variety of systems lends itself to a variety of uses, and divergent classifications entail clashes of interpretation.[29] A pointed example is the use of texts as examples and illustrations in course design. It is for reasons such as these that the habitual separation of 'use' and 'interpretation' is futile: the systems of possible classification for any text are exactly the domains of its possible use. While the number of such classificatory systems is in principle unlimited, it is one of the implications of the theory of discursive formations that they are limited in practice. It is practice, after all, that we are after. Nevertheless, the practical implication of the 'in principle' clause is that the classifications of a given text are an open set, and it is this that explains the necessary inadequacy of any particular taxonomy of genres.

When Derrida expounded the paradoxes of the law of genre – that the metageneric is generic to genre, and that heterogeneity is germane to the claim to homogeneity – there were those who took this up as spelling the end of genre theory and putting paid to the very postulate of genre. I have chosen to do otherwise. Granted that, if texts are filed in multiple and heterogeneous systems, it would be futile for genre theory to attempt to reduce these to a single system of categories. Granted, equally, that all attempts to correlate a system of generic labels with a system of semiotic properties must therefore fail. Indeed, it follows analytically from the claim that the metageneric is generic to genre that it is not a theoretical metalanguage, if what we mean by a theoretical metalanguage is just that it is not generic to its object. But the postulate of genre is not dissolved by these paradoxes. In them, 'genre' is all the more insistent. In these circumstances, the task of a theory of genre might be to provide strategies of analysis of the intrication of a text in the systems deployed to classify it, of the operations of these systems as they determine use, and of their clash, their intersection, or their complicity in the guidance and the governance of semiosis.[30]

THE THEORY OF A GENRE

In literary circles, for the greater part of a century, it has been possible to relegate the question of genre to the margins of theory, either – with the New Critics – in the name of the uniqueness of the individual text, or – with the structuralists and the deconstructionists – in the name of the general processes of signification which are said to function with equal complexity across the full range of semiotic artefacts. A parallel marginalizing of genre is documented by Paul Willemen and Stephen Neale in respect of its place in film theory.[31]

It is not enough to signal, triumphantly, the return of genre from across these margins of the radically individual and the radically general. It is necessary to spell out why genre matters. To this end, the linguists have offered a mediation of the dichotomy of the individual and the social by breaking up the notion of 'language' with that of local and functionally specific codes and protocols mapped on to 'social situations'. Likewise, in the work on film, where debates have been significantly inflected by psychoanalysis, the notion of genre has offered an alternative to the same dichotomy by considering 'signification in terms of modes of address and discursive strategies', these being understood as constructive of 'instances of subjectivity'.[32] In both these places, the focus has come to rest on the micro-politics of particular genres.

Give or take the minor matter of whether to define the 'unconscious' as a social automatism or as a site in the Freudian topology, these two annexations of the notion of genre share the assumption that a genre functions independently of any consciously deployed knowledge on the part of the (speaking or viewing) subject. On this assumption, the point of a theory is modelled on the aims of what is now a classical linguistics: it is to produce a set of self-consistent and adequate premises for the description of particular genres, it being understood that such a description is the explication of rules that are effectively operative at the unconscious, or deep-structural, level. Theory comes from an elsewhere to provide a metalanguage in which a genre will be called to account, and Known.

To think this is what a theory of genre should look like, and to persist in proposing new and improved models thereof, betokens an astonishing faith in the epistemological project of a theoretical metalanguage – not to mention a failure to recognize the generic specificity of classification itself, or the place of metageneric descriptions in, and not outside, 'the law of genre'.

Let me be plain. I have mentioned two sites at which metageneric descriptions arise: the text, which locates itself generically in relation to other texts by means of like- and not-statements; and filing systems. There is a third, which we might for the sake of convenience call the critical commentary. There is every good reason for not treating this as a genre *à part entière*. Each genre, I should argue, throws up the possibility of its own appropriate kind of commentary, leading to the hypothesis that uptake is doubled by a reading of this aestheticizing kind. Here is an example: imagine the appropriate mode of reception of a sermon. Members of the congregation do not interact; they sit, not kneel or stand; they neither produce nor reproduce ritual or spontaneous discourse; heads are bowed in the posture of interiority, or eyes are raised to the preacher in the posture of inspiration; it is a silent but no doubt articulate discourse of, say, moral reflection, perhaps mimicking the preacher's strategies of quotation and exemplification. Rebellion and doubt are not excluded, but they are in due form. This is uptake. But, once outside the church, in the social forms of greeting and exchange that bind the congregation in different but equally effective ways as a community, say, of parishioners – standing, talking, and in eye contact with one another, with the preacher in third-person position – the faithful are apt to become critics. 'He spoke so well again today, don't you think?' 'Not like the old days. His father had such a way with words.' 'A fine use of the text . . .' 'I didn't agree with his interpretation of . . .' 'I wish he'd stop bringing in politics. That's not what I'd call a sermon!'

Whether sports or political commentary, arts criticism, conversation about conversations, bus tickets, or advertisements,[33] such texts can be understood as fulfilling the classificatory and normative functions associated with classic genre theory – with this difference: that each is germane to its own object-genre. Each is generic. At least some of the rules of any genre are made explicit in this entirely conscious evaluative move: the commentary of a text includes – may *be* – the theory of its genre. This is a hypothesis that I cannot develop further here, but I adumbrate my intention to pursue it in further work. If, as I suppose, such commentaries spell out the protocols of their genres, they have a systematic teaching-and-learning function. It is not the job of genre theory to do likewise. Rather, I would require of theoretical intervention in the matter of genre that it investigate this process and its strategies.[34] The normativity of genre cannot be dismissed in the libertarian hope that it will go away. Appropriate uptake may well be boring for the boffins of artistic creativity, but it entails a theory of the inappropriate, the criterion for the mis-take. Mistakes matter: they are the moments of the local or general, provisional or definitive, trivial or crucial losses of the place of speech. Genre is the site of the regulation of the power over, as well as the power of, discourse.

It is a commonplace in arts criticism, for example, that a text can exert pressure on its generic boundaries and elicit a commentary that attempts to exclude it from the class to which it lays such paradoxical claim. Witness our apolitical congregant. Such moments of conflict are frequently given the status of events signalling generic change, and are cited as evidence for the argument that constitutive rules are necessarily also regulative. The division of labour of these two functions may correspond to the distinction between the text and its commentary. It is important not to confuse them, nor to forget their profound complicity. In this regard, another useful job that genre theory could do would be to investigate the differences between the operations of not-statements as they are made in a text about itself, and those made by a commentary about an object-text. For, whereas the not-statement of the text is a stratagem for laying claim to a place adjacent to but not identical with a number of named others, the not-statement of the commentary refuses to acknowledge that claim. It withholds uptake, and by so doing deprives the text of any generic status and disempowers it. Not-statements are not merely descriptive propositions; they are discursive acts committed in territorial combat.

This is the struggle for entitlement. Our hold on it is precarious, and subject to sanction. If commentaries are the mechanism for teaching a genre, we might also ponder on schooling as the organized site for the deployment of commentary. Most of the foregoing argument first appeared in a paper entitled 'Anyone for tennis?' which was my response to a brief. It has lost the frame which gave it its place, and it has lost its title. *Perdre ses titres*, in French, means to lose one's accreditation for acting in a professionally or institutionally defined place. In this situation, one might suppose, I should be casting around in a discursive void, in urgent need of another assignment. But to lose one's place is simply, and automatically, to be somewhere else. My paper was not a game, I said in the lost place; it was a move in a game. It was itself an uptake, and it expected an uptake. Its title was an invitation to that effect, addressed to the work in curriculum and syllabus design that gives a place to genre theory. Here I throw down the gauntlet in another arena. In the lost place, I considered the place of genre in learning; here I frame the question of the place of teaching in genre.

University of Queensland

Notes

I wish to thank the following people for their comments and suggestions in response to an earlier draft of this paper: Jennifer Craik and Frances Oppel, of Griffith University; John Macarthur and James Wheatley, of Queensland University; and Laurie Gaffney, of Curriculum Services, Queensland Department of Education – great tennis-players, all.

1 Michael Reddy, 'The conduit metaphor', in A. Ortony (ed.), *Metaphor and Thought* (Cambridge: Cambridge University Press, 1970), pp. 284–324.
2 Ludwig Wittgenstein, *Philosophical Investigations*, trans. G. E. M. Anscombe (Oxford: Basil Blackwell, 1953), sec. 23. The notion has been taken up and its use extended by Jean-François Lyotard, *The Postmodern Condition: A Report on Knowledge*, trans. Geoff Bennington and Brian Massumi, Foreword by Fredric Jameson (Minneapolis: University of Minnesota Press, 1984).
3 Cf. Tzvetan Todorov, *Les Genres du discours* (Paris: Seuil, 1978); Mikhail Bakhtin and Valentin Vološinov, *Marxism and the Philosophy of Language*, trans. L. Matejka and I. R. Titunik (New York: Seminar Press, 1973). Jacques Derrida assumes the continuity of the two notions in his critique, 'The law of genre', *Glyph*, 7 (1980), pp. 176–201.
4 J. L. Austin, *How to do Things with Words* (Cambridge, Mass.: Harvard University Press, 1967).
5 Cf. Mary-Louise Pratt, *Towards a Speech-Act Theory of Literary Discourse* (Bloomington: Indiana University Press, 1977).
6 John Searle, *Speech Acts* (1969; Cambridge: Cambridge University Press, 1978).
7 M. A. K. Halliday, *Language as Social Semiotic* (London: Edward Arnold, 1978). Cf. the use made of Halliday's work by John Frow, 'Discourse genres', *Journal of Literary Semantics*, 9, 2 (1980), pp. 73–81, and more recently by Gunther Kress, *Linguistic Processes in Sociocultural Practice* (Deakin University, 1985) and 'Socio-linguistic development and the mature language user: different voices for different occasions', in G. Sells and J. Nicholls (eds), *Language Learning: An Interactional Perspective* (Lewes: Falmer Press, 1985). Cf. also J. Martin and Joan Rothery, *Writing Project Report*, Working Papers in Linguistics, no. 1 (Linguistics Department, University of Sydney, 1980). Halliday, as distinct from some of his followers, does invoke the notion 'the semiotic system that constitutes the culture' (quoted in Frow, op. cit., p. 73), but the assumption that this is a *single* system, coupled with the failure to investigate its operations, results in a reduction of this notion to those of 'context' and 'situation'. This is a simple text/context model, where 'text' is the output of two sets of rules, linguistic and social. To name the latter 'social semiotic' changes very little in practice. For a critique of the notion of 'register' in terms of its inadequacy to deal with 'genre', see Ian Reid, 'A register of deaths?', to appear in T. and J. Burton (eds), *Linguistic and Lexicographical Studies: Essays in Honour of G. W. Turner* (London: Boydell & Brewer, 1987).
8 Note that this requirement is not included in the notion that the rules of a game are the rules governing the pieces (e.g. of chess) and the uses to which they can be put. Cf. Lyotard, op. cit., p. 10, glossing Wittgenstein.
9 This claim is made on the basis of arguments contesting the place of 'discourse' in a model of the generation of texts, but *mutatis mutandis* holds for genre as well. See David Lee, 'Discourse: does it hang together?', typescript in circulation.
10 William H. Davis, *Peirce's Epistemology* (The Hague: Martinus Nijhoff, 1972), p. vii.
11 *The Pocket Oxford Dictionary* (1924), rev. edn (Oxford: Oxford University Press, 1955), preface to the first edition.
12 Ferdinand de Saussure, *Course in General Linguistics*, ed. C. Bally and A. Sèchehaye in collaboration with A. Reidlinger, trans. W. Baskin (New York: McGraw-Hill, 1966).
13 Martin Buzacott, *Charivari* (Sydney: Picador, 1987), p. 8.

14 Australian Department of Immigration and Ethnic Affairs application for entry for settlement, form M 47 (8–78) 14, attachment 1, chapter 12, front of form.

15 This discussion of Balzac relies heavily on Christopher Prendergast, *The Order of Mimesis* (Cambridge: Cambridge University Press, 1986), ch. 3.

16 Gertrude Stein, *Three Lives*, Signet Classics (New York: New American Library, 1985).

17 Umberto Eco, *The Name of the Rose*, trans. William Weaver (London: Picador, 1984).

18 Eudora Welty, *The Ponder Heart* (London: Virago, 1983), p. 51.

19 Honoré de Balzac, *Le Père Goriot*, Livre de Poche (Paris: Gallimard, 1972), pp. 5–6.

20 This point takes as its premise Peter Cryle's use of the apartment block as the central thematic figure in his discussion of nineteenth-century French prose fiction, in the course he runs on that topic in the Department of French, University of Queensland.

21 John Berger, 'Imagine Paris', *Good Weekend: The Sydney Morning Herald Weekend Magazine*, 28 February 1987, pp. 42–5.

22 I am grateful to Joanna Peters for this point.

23 See Richard Paterson, 'Planning the family: the art of the television schedule', *Screen Education*, 35 (Summer 1980), pp. 79–85.

24 Such genres are, however, included in John Frow's categorization of discourse genres (op. cit., p. 75).

25 For this point in relation to photography, see Helen Grace, 'To the Lighthouse', in Virginia Coventry (ed.), *The Critical Distance* (Sydney: Hale & Ironmonger, 1982), pp. 112–19, and, in relation to literary narrative, see Ian Reid, 'Reading frames for literary learning', to appear in the *Proceedings of the Australian Reading Association* (Sydney, July 1987).

26 Paper read to the Architecture School, University of Queensland, on 3 March 1987.

27 This is my uptake of Derrida's argument (op. cit.; cf. note 3).

28 An example I have used elsewhere for other purposes is that of Foucault's *The Archaeology of Knowledge*, first catalogued by the Library of Congress as 'archeology' (cf. Anne Freadman, 'Riffatera cognita: a late contribution to the formalism debate', *Substance*, 42 (1983), pp. 31–45.

29 Cf. John Frow, *Marxism and Literary History* (Cambridge, Mass.: Harvard University Press, 1986), ch. 8.

30 Here again I follow the argument of John Frow, in ibid.

31 Stephen Neale, *Genre* (London: British Film Institute, 1980/1983); presentation by Paul Willemen.

32 Ibid., pp. 4 and 7.

33 The point can be made most forcefully in respect of forms, where an 'applied semiotics' has been brought to bear on their design on the basis of the criterion of cost-effectiveness. See David Sless, 'Repairing messages: the hidden cost of inappropriate theory', *Australian Journal of Communications*, 9 and 10 (1986), pp. 82–93, esp. 89 ff.

34 Cf. Ian Hunter, 'Culture and government: the emergence of literary education', PhD thesis (Griffith University, 1986). Hunter's argument is far broader in scope, and does not rely particularly on the notion of genre. Nevertheless, the role of literary criticism in the schooling strategies he describes lends itself to redescription in these terms.

LESLEY STERN

PHOTOS BY KEVIN BALLANTINE

CUP CITY: WHERE NOTHING ENDS, NOTHING HAPPENS

S ee in your mind's eye a body posturing, imagine a posture of anticipation, a posture of arrival. The pose, the posture, the gesture – these are processes, movements of the body, of bodies in relation to other bodies; an arena of proxemics, of energy.

Imagine a perfect location.

Look at these images. Two views: a beach of sorts, a cluster of possibly urban buildings. They could be anywhere, any place, this beach, these buildings; there is nothing in the photographs to render the particularity of Place. No landmarks, no familiar iconography, no human interest. If photographs are inescapably descriptive, as some would have it, then these are perversely nondescript. They evoke the ideality of Anywhere or Nowhere. If the photograph is documentation, why do we not instantly recognize these views as the Being of Place? From one perspective it's because nothing takes place (so more is happening than just the ellipsis of iconography). There is no obvious happening, no promise of eventuality, no incipient drama. There is an erasure of the figurative (in the still photograph drama is always only incipient, projected as a potential, or a trace, in the spacing of bodies and things, the rendering of Space into Place).

Yet, even if place is elusive, space figures insistently in both these views.

The America's Cup, an international yachting competition held in Fremantle, Western Australia, over the summer of 1986–7, was orchestrated, and for the most part presented, as an epic event. It was also a nationalistic event, since Australia was defending the Cup, wrested last time round from the Americans,who had long held both the title and the location for the race. Alan Bond, a local-boy-made-good (read millions), was both skipper of the main Australian boat and prime mover of entrepreneurial activities associated with the event. It was an event staged, like many sporting and competitive events, for a particular kind of rendition – 'live coverage' (with television as the agency of presence for those not fortunate

enough to be participating observers). For more than a year before the happening, media publicity was geared towards a fostering of anticipation – anticipation of suspense, primarily; also, anticipation of Fremantle as a tourist utopia. Fremantle: a venue for street theatre, for the festive conjugality of flamboyant entrepreneurs and discreet aristocrats; Fremantle as a carnivalesque setting where international yachties would walk in step with sunloving and barefooted locals, a setting at once cosmopolitan and cosy, worldly and casual. The ocean was anticipated as both backdrop to this tourist extravaganza and as focus of attention, a screen for the projection of spectacle, excitement, suspense.

There is something shocking, arresting, about this series of photos taken during the Cup.[1] There is not a yacht in sight. These images do not correspond to the Fremantle we had been led to expect, or even the Fremantle we remember from the media, especially television. Not only are there no yachts; there is no colour, and the series suggests an air of languid immobility. There are few people and lots of space. The figures that do appear seem to have been left over from some other photographic event. They are hanging around as though waiting for something to happen. They are watchful (though not of the camera) and awkward in their desultory vigilance. These photos do not invoke spectacle, excitement, suspense.

To turn again to those views where space figures so insistently.

The path to the beach is paved with civilized intention. There is a skinny strip of sea that obtrudes across a fraction of the frame somewhere towards the top. A bit of sand and a few tussocks lurk in the centre. On the horizon, between the sea and the sky – something that looks like a ship. It is not simply the mass of the foreground that affronts the gaze; an expanse of sand would be expansive and picturesque. No, it is the civility inscribed in stone, in stone slabs laid as a margin between the imaginary but obdurate texture of tarmac and the vagaries of sand and wind. For these stones are a testimony to emptiness, to space – a space unfilled by people. If there were bits of litter or footprints, we could read in the emptiness an inscription of presence, a murmuring of desolation. But there is no sense of abandonment here, just the banality of an empty barren space.

A paved courtyard, a space for strolling. A dense layer of shadow covers the ground. Arising out of this shadow mass, an edging of buildings, sharp angles and curved awnings, bright clean surfaces, a pristine palm tree. No people and, again, no litter. The sense of intimacy generic to the courtyard scene is both evoked and mocked by the dense triangular slab of space that grounds the composition, by the scrupulosity of cleanliness. Yet there is a detail that perturbs. In a window we can see a building ladder propped against another window. The depth of focus paradoxically renders this detail obscure. Is it a reflection of a ladder just out of view, or is it a ladder seen through the window, situated in an empty space lurking behind the building's façade? What it does suggest, either way, is an air not of abandonment but of prematurity. It is too soon to look through the window. For what we see pictured here is on one level a familiar transnational style of architecture – a 'West Coast' hybrid or televisual Miami. Yet it is distinctly a Miami without vice. It's a film set not quite ready for the action.

To situate these two photographs as an 'opening' (as the instigation for a sequence) is obviously a loaded manoeuvre. They are unavoidably set up to frame the images that follow, to set the scene. They are bound to restrain, to put into place the mechanisms for reconciling time and space. Yet in the presentation of still photographs (as opposed to film or writing) a contradiction, precisely between time and space, is played out against the impulse to anticipate. If the articulation of time and space (mostly notably in dreams, but in other forms of narrative too) locates *difference* as much as *continuity*, this is nowhere more evident than in the sequencing of still photographs. It is to possible dislocations that I want to look. And to do so I want to anticipate the projection of two possible scenarios and to suggest a third.

Given the known context of these photographs, it would be possible to read these two images as having a narrative motivation. This reading would be less concerned with the apparently idiosyncratic perspective of the photographer (in comparison with other representations of the Cup – filled with teeming life and streamlined technology) and would read the evocation of empty space as a narrative pretext. Expectation would be inscribed into the space, an expectation that an event (the Cup, the spectating) will take place, that this will effect a filling of the emptiness, a transformation of space into place. This reading prefigures the figurative, for it anticipates action and actants. These images, then, suggest suspense. The second potential scenario is more grounded in metaphor and an impulse to thematization. This perspective renders these images familiar – not as a particular place, but as the representation of a metaphor. The dead centre, the inland sea, the empty heart, the barren waste that is Australia is read into these images so that they become evocations of a generalized place – *terra nullius*. This reading also transforms space into place but inscribes suspense not as temporal but as immanent.

Holding these two potential scenarios in mind, I want to explore a third. Let me complicate two terms already invoked – space and place – by introducing notions of 'location' and the 'perfect location fallacy'. I borrow the term 'location' from cinematic practice, where it is used to indicate a 'real' environment where filming takes place, as distinct from a studio and the paraphernalia of studio sets. It is used in association with fiction more often than with documentary, for in the letter the environment does not readily present itself as a potential *mise-en-scène*.

When Raul Ruiz, the film maker, was asked 'Why do you make films?' he replied:

le cinéma m'est toujours apparu comme l'expression la plus parfaite de la 'perfect location fallacy' (A. N. Whitehead). D'après ses principes, il y a toujours une place qui est mieux qu'une autre pour placer un object et il y en a une de parfaite par objet. L'ennui, avec le cinéma, c'est qu'on perd beaucoup de temps à la chercher et que toutes les places, au hasard, ont l'air parfaites.[2]

The perfect location exists only in imagination. Yet it is not non-existent. The traces of desire (for a perfect *mise-en-scène*, staging of objects and bodies in a signifying space) are found in the event of filmic images, in the imaginary of fiction. What we have (what we see?) in the event is not an absence of perfection, but traces of dislocation.

Location, in the filmic sense, is not habitually used in the realm of still photography, perhaps because of the force (even if only residual) of documentation. However, in the collision between Ruiz and Ballantine a collusion is generated, and the 'perfect location fallacy' appears as strikingly pertinent to still photography. This collection of photos suggests Fremantle/Perth as a location in at least two, overlapping, senses. First, the photographic process explores and documents another process – the social/historical siting of the Cup in this location. In this filtering of processes, what we see is not the perfect location but traces of the search, an imaging of the perfect location fallacy. Hence, not an absence of crowds, yachts, and so on, but a tracing of dislocation between place and the anticipatory imaging of that place in the hysteria of media hype. Secondly, Fremantle/Perth is deployed as a location for the imaginary of fiction. Because still photographers don't generally go on location hunts with a script under their arm, we might assume they are not motivated by desire for the perfect location. Yet why should we assume that they are not driven by a search for the perfect location as that space where everything falls into place, as that place which is better than any other for situating objects, items, ideas, dreams? In different ways the sea and the factory have provided pretexts for the development of documentary genres of photography, yet simultaneously these very genres can be read as projections of the imaginary. So perhaps the concept of location – as both a siting and the potential for a staging, for a *mise-en-scène* – is pertinent to all photography. What interests me particularly in these Ballantine photos is the convergence of a desire to site with an impulse to citation.

A beach, a cluster of buildings – empty space. These images (reading to and fro between these and other images in the series) cite the *idea* of location as an arena of the imaginary. In their figuring out of space (and erasure of the figurative) they suggest not so much a particularity of place as a potential for photographic rendering. That potential is evoked in a diffusion between the materiality of the representation and the abstraction. These images evoke the 'perfect location' (for a particular photographic rendition) at the very moment when they inscribe the fallacy of perfection. The series as a whole reminds me of Freud's description of the unconscious as a location where 'nothing ends, nothing happens, nothing is forgotten'. But particularly in these opening images, which set the scene for a photographic staging in which the desire of the photographer (and the viewer) renders space into place, and, more acutely, place into space.

To read these images as a citation of siting is to displace to some extent the 'narrative pretext' reading. The empty space is not loaded with expectation or suspense. However, it would be brashly precipitous to refuse all entertainment of suspense. This series of photographs is located (by this writing, by other media images) and contextualized by an extravagantly rhetorical event. A rhetoric of suspense and anticipation was integral to the production of this event as a contemporary commercial epic. Ballantine's photos deploy their own rhetoric to infiltrate, diffuse, and defuse the rhetoric of the epic.

And what of the metaphoric? Can we fill these images with all the plenitude that the void, the empty heart of Australia, has to offer? The metaphoric is enticing, yet I think the photos resist such a reading in their deflection of the familiar. The image of Australia as an uninhabited and hostile space is an image that exactly renders place into space. As has often been pointed out, it is a white colonial rendering (a whitewash job), an image conceived by urban eyes. Colin Johnson has observed that it is not entirely a reactive image; it is also a perversely imaginative projection:

> Terra Nullius, that heart of emptiness, has always been sought to be filled by the European . . . by a huge inland sea [a fantasy of early explorers] reflecting what else but the coast of Australia, representing what else but the familiar, especially the British familiar, the island familiar, the sound of the sea, the taste of the sea, the sight of the ocean never far from their senses, until a mind reality must be projected into suitable emptiness.

Further:

> A land people would not have dreamed a sea where none existed, nor would they have pictured all that is land as being a wide dreary beach edging on to the true reality of a sea.[3]

A curiously insular imagination, then, an anachronistically imperial insularity, produces this resonating metaphor (which still multiplies and reverberates in those endless lists disgorged by the ubiquitous postmodern pasticheur).

Johnson's perspective provides an apt framing for the reflective process of Ballantine's series. So we can read the images of people looking out to sea (where nothing appears to happen) and the emptiness of the ocean as projected back into the urban landscape. Thus the photographic event (as opposed to the Cup event) is not devoid of metaphoric trace, but it is not the predictable metaphor that frames the emptiness. For if these photos conjure Fremantle as an imaginary location they are also and simultaneously (through the process of the series) a documentation of place. Not a documentation of an event (though the event provides a dimension of fictionality), but of a place, perceived as a constellation of traits. There are none of the usual media landmarks – pavement cafés pulsating with cosmopolitan atmosphere, overflowing and convivial pubs, quaintly rejigged buildings, meticulously restored façades. But this is undoubtedly an urban coastal landscape. The landscape is austere, sparse, composed in a gauchely *ad hoc* manner – but the urban is imprinted in every composition. And, if the images are ghosted by the America's Cup, so too they are haunted by another Fremantle, never pictured as such. Fremantle is a port town: its immediate coast is industrialized, it is historically a place of arrivals and

departures, a point of exit and of destination. On the edge of Perth (linked by sprawling suburbia), it is also on the far edge of the continent, facing towards the Indian Ocean rather than the rest of Australia. Perth is nowadays also the home of those who have 'arrived' – the self-made millionaires, the nationalistic sporting tycoons – and of those who are always about to leave (sacrilegiously ungratified by the laid-back lifestyle) in search of a 'real' city.

So people hang around in these photos, never quite arriving or departing, in transit yet poised, in vague expectation of movement, of something happening. They look out to sea and appear to see bugger all. If there are yachts out there, there is no sense of a race, no sense of departure and arrival, nothing happens, nothing ends. If letters always reach their destination, yachts, it would seem, are curiously suspended and imaginary. And yet the Cup, as an event (that takes place through duration), is inscribed in these still photographs in the configuration of urban space. It is not the desert that is imprinted in this space; it is the ocean as location of an imaginary epic event.

An immaculate Norfolk pine is planted dead centre. In the top half of the frame: sky. In the bottom half: paving stones. A discrete slash of ocean separates the elements. Off-centre a second tree, diminished by perspective but in perfect symmetry with the centre. A hard dark shadow is cast jaggedly on the paving stones by a suspended rubbish bin. Is it there as a repository for pine needles which might escape composure and contaminate the unsullied surface? But then is it a real pine tree? Perhaps the set has been cleared, all litter already deposited in the bin; or perhaps the bin is a sign of anticipation, a premonition of untidy tourists. Are we seeing a real location that is like a set, or a set that is preparing for the real?

In the distance, reduced out of proportion, a corporate toy town. Presiding over these miniature buildings, an austere yet menacing sprinkler. An ungainly tree lurches sideways, away from buildings and sprinkler. Is this prehensile watering device located here to nurture the expansive grassy foreground, or to put a damper over the city? Is this an appropriate place for an epic event?

A souvenir kiosk in the middle of nowhere. A prefab, hired, temporary structure; backed on to the foreshore, it faces a clean and empty road. A large litter bin stands waiting. The paving, the road, the litter bin – all testify to an urban location, yet, simultaneously, to a forlorn lack of urbanity. There is a sense of anonymity (Nowhere or Anywhere) evoked by the composition, a sense that persists, pervasive, despite the declaration of place. 'G'day' – an Australian colloquialism, a greeting, a hello – becomes incorporated into a declaration of Western Australian identity/hospitality. Functioning as a slogan of the euphemistic 'hospitality industry', it renders local identity equally euphemistic. It appears, compelled by the force of repetition, in the most inhospitable configurations: in symmetry with other repetitions – sale, sale, sale – and inscribed on T-shirts worn by headless mannequins posing behind glass windows.

Writing figures more insistently in many of these photos than does the human figure. Yet what is traced in the textual is not the absence of human

agency but the presence of advertising. It is there in the Coke bottle neatly exposed in a bin of scrupulously bagged and concealed rubbish, and on Alan Bond's airship advertising the product of his brewery – Swan Premium.

During the Cup, the airship, in marked contrast to seagoing ships or yachts, was ever-present and ever-visible, circling the air, signalling an event. Here it figures incongruously, grounded like an ignominious whale, in the bush. No clearer image could there be of a re-placing of the ocean epic.

Other writings, more playful and more deadly, are inscribed in the photographic space. The Bond building is underwritten by graffiti: 'Fathers are the danger *not* the stranger'. In the context of a series on the Cup, the paternal might be inflected as the menace of City Fathers, of corporate capital; incest and domestic cannibalism as more immediately threatening than sporting competitors. Cannibalism surfaces elsewhere (where else but on T-shirts?) in a possibly more playful mode – 'Dennis Conner Eats Kiwis'. If it is playful, it is only so because the intelligibility of the slogan depends upon a posturing of Siamese twins. Yet, after Arbus (and after the Bond building), how can this posture avoid traces of sinister discomfort.

A solitary woman with her back to the camera holds binoculars to her eyes and looks out to sea. Her body is settled to support the raising of her arms; she is entirely focused on the activity of looking, appears settled in this posture as though she has grown into it, waiting. Although we do not see the binoculars, they are imaginatively present, evoked through gesturality.

Similarly, the sea is scarcely present. We can imagine its being there, but what she actually sees is entirely in the realm of the imaginary. The view of the binoculars and the view of the camera do not coincide.

They look in different directions, these watchers, shoulders averted, glances crossing. A haphazardly formed group clusters, anticipating an arrival, but from where, and what is it that will happen? They appear to be suspended in transit, perhaps at a bus stop, perhaps awaiting a message from the sky. A woman, rising out of the sea, arrives in an empty space, glances towards an empty chair on the edge of the frame. She clutches a towel to her body as though pausing, shielding herself awkwardly from a hostile view. The same location, but peopled, people coming and going, turning their backs on the ocean. A group of three men, arrested in a moment of confidentiality, of body confidence.

Nothing appears to be happening out there on the ocean. Nothing begins or ends. And yet in the photographic scene nothing (of what is happening out there) is forgotten. If the America's Cup, in the event, turned out to be an impossible vision, impossible as a spectator sport, the imaginary of the event is imprinted in the photographic space. These hapless spectators see something: instead of yachts they see 'G'day from WA'. They will leave eventually, bereft of photos, documentation of an epic event enacted by a cast of thousands; but they will go bearing souvenirs, memories of the place inscribed on their bodies, on T-shirts which they will wear out.

If the image of an ocean event occurs as an impression imprinted on T-shirts (and in empty space), this process involves both deflection and reduction. While the photographic process evokes generalized reflections upon the 'perfect location fallacy', the elision betwen spectatorship and tourism, it also documents, in a quite specific way, the relation between space and place and dimension. The siting of Fremantle/Perth involves a perception of the way in which small cities (particularly cities small in population and large in terms of space) project their own identity by reducing everything (starting with litter, with foreign contamination), by an impulse to scale down. So the Bond building finds its reflection in a tacky makeshift kiosk. But, obversely, the photographic process projects the tawdriness of souvenirs back into the site of entrepreneurial pretension.

There is one photograph in the series which shows a group of people, suspenseful, all looking intently in the same direction. The location is a pub and their necks are craned, their eyes cast upwards. Following their gaze, where do we arrive? An expansive ceiling, the whirr of a fan immobilized rendering atmosphere tactile, an invitation to travel – Air New Zealand – propped in a corner. And in the centre, at the bottom of the frame but close to the ceiling: a television set. There are images there in the small screen, a sense of crowding, of activity. But what are those images? We can only imagine.

Perth, 1987

Notes

1 I have made a small selection from the series. Kevin Ballantine has made a different (though sometimes overlapping) selection for an exhibition held in Perth in September 1987.
2 *Liberation* (May 1987).
3 Colin Johnson, 'A sea of dreams; a rock of reality; a land of travel', unpublished paper.

JOHN HARTLEY

A STATE OF EXCITEMENT: WESTERN AUSTRALIA AND THE AMERICA'S CUP

The familiar radical slogan is: THINK GLOBALLY; ACT LOCALLY. This advice was not so much subverted as inverted during the 1986–7 America's Cup in Western Australia – the trick was to act globally but think locally.

The Cup, an event induced by media, attracting 2,000 visiting journalists and creating a new meaning for Western Australia in the eyes of the world's television, generated more than euphoric images of Australia, sport, and leisure for American tourists. It provoked, within the host community, an unwonted but sustained bout of self-reflexivity and utopianism. It became the mechanism – or rather the practice – through which questions of national (or quasi-national) identity and signification could be thought through; it was a race against time, space, and structure.

What follows can be read as a review of some aspects of an exotic local event; equally, however, it can be seen as an account of an increasingly international cultural/political phenomenon – the *euphoricization* of democracy and the mobilization of national unity as a commodity to sell on the open market of the consciousness industries within a global economy of commodified meaning.

Within this economy, the distinctions between texts and contexts disappear; the bodies and actions of the people involved (which is everybody) are *textualized* into a cultural practice of competitive performance: to put the local on show for the global – to *act* globally.

A state of excitement

Western Australia is a sign in need of a referent. The size of western Europe with the population of, say, greater Croydon, it is the site of mines and other holes in the ground,[1] surrounded by, well, nothing. Its metropolis, Perth – according to a 1986 advertisement broadcast on local television on behalf of the Roy Weston Real Estate company (the 'HouseSold Name in Real Estate') – is the 'loneliest, most isolated capital city in the world'.

After the America's Cup, Western Australia displays, in defeat, questions. It is characterized by space, emptiness, isolation, disequilibrium, enigma. Its history is of successive immigrations – rushes – followed by disappointment, stagnation, regression – depopulation. Founded in 1829, it still has more immigrants from overseas or over east than native-born citizens. Successively, land areas and specific means of economic exploitation are worked out; mines are abandoned, forests are felled, crops are swallowed up in salt and sand. People are reminded that they belong elsewhere. They go. Some go, some die.[2]

The questions aroused by the America's Cup, by another cycle of rush, defeat, and depopulation, are, like Western Australia's industries, *primary* ones. They're not 'What kind of a place is WA?'; not 'How do people look at it?' Those are interpretative, value-added questions, relying on the familiar manufacturing processes of realist intellection where signs and discourses are combined with referents in an expanding, self-sustaining economy of knowledge. But such questions, which concentrate on fitting suitable fictions to known facts, presuppose the prior existence of primary referents. For Western Australia, this would be incautious; here, the primary questions are 'Is it?'; 'Is there anything to look at?'; 'Is there anyone to look?'

Of course, there's a land mass and a population. But, just as the state's economy has not, as yet, achieved integration, complexity, or self-sustaining expansion, so the land mass and population are not, as yet, integrated into a sign that self-evidently proclaims 'Western Australianness'. They have not achieved legibility within an economy of coherence. Like the slogans on the state's vehicle licence plates, which proclaim WA as the 'Home of the America's Cup', or the 'State of Excitement', they are pure signs, uncontaminated by referents.

In the familiar, white, Western economy of knowledge, Western Australia must be tamed, shorn of its realities and then spun and woven into realism; it must be transformed from nature to culture. As it stands, it cannot *stand for*; to white, Western eyes, it is a giant, fearful, unthinkable Other – the only remaining vestige, perhaps, of the old imperial Heart of Darkness, 'the horror, the horror'.[3] In an entirely appropriate exchange of symbols, after the America's Cup, victory is – literally – swallowed up in death. A representative of culture in the shape of a 24-year-old American part-time model, partaking of the ultimate tourist experience, has attended the Cup event, and is now cruising round the Kimberley coast in the state's far north-west, accessible only by sea. She stops for a swim (or perhaps the call of nature) under the falls on the Prince Regent River. In a latterday version of 'The convergence of the twain', the 'grotesque, slimed, dumb, indifferent' representative of nature, in the shape of a large crocodile, queries 'What does this vaingloriousness down here?'[4] The weapons of culture, in the shape of a shoe hurled at the crocodile's head, do not prevail; the woman is, as the local euphemism has it, 'taken'.

But horror is not confined to the natural world in Western Australia; it suffuses the social world too, both public and private. Just as the competing crews were taking a few days off over Christmas 1986 for resting and rorting, there was another death, in Perth. A 25-year-old Murdoch University student had been imprisoned for a month for driving while under suspension. In prison he fell ill. As is customary in Western Australia, the prison authorities assumed he was under the influence of illicit liquor or illegal drugs. So it was only after some days that he was taken, dying, to hospital. Although he was delirious and had only five days of a sentence for a victimless, minor traffic offence to serve, he was, as is the custom in Western Australia, shackled to his hospital bed with a stainless-steel leg-iron, and guarded by two warders. No one from the prison bothered to inform his mother. Her comment, as given to *The Sydney Morning Herald* (18 April 1987) was: 'Nothing can justify the State being worse than the worst among us. It was the most barbaric thing I have ever seen – something you wouldn't inflict on the wildest, most brutal animal.' In the same *Herald* story, Tony Vinson, Professor of Social Work at the University of New South Wales and former head of that state's Corrective Services Department, said that the 'very common' custom, in WA, of chaining sick prisoners to their hospital beds, no matter what their crime or condition, was 'medieval and barbaric': 'It's something that is practised by no other country that pretends to be nearly civilised. I cannot find words to express my horror.'

And horror visits the private sector too, in this State of Excitement. Two boys, aged 16 and 17, who were employed to look after two giant cattle stations in the state's north-west, disappeared just as the finalists for the America's Cup defence and challenge were sorting themselves out. Five months later, the boys' bodies were found, one with a bullet hole in the skull, on the edge of the Great Sandy Desert. Their Datsun 'ute' had become bogged down, and there was little they could do but walk, sit under trees whose shade may have reduced the daytime temperature to around 50°C, and then either wait for, or hasten, death. Why were they there? It seems they were running away – from reputed beatings with stockwhips, routine violence alternating with unremitting labour and long periods of complete isolation on the otherwise unmanned cattle stations. They may also have been afraid of getting into trouble for taking the Datsun for their flight. No one saw them, and no one imagined they would take the route they did, so the search planes, while covering an area the size of the state of Victoria, missed them. This was the fate of two school-leavers, one from South Australia and one from New South Wales, who had no reason to know what life as a 'jackaroo' in WA was like, and no training to deal with it. They had simply answered an ad in the paper.

Such is the potential reality of WA, the limit-case of the referent. Small wonder, among this gigantism, inhumanity, and horror, to find that knowledge of it, constructed into a realist coherence, is not what characterizes its discourses. On the contrary, and necessarily, Western Australia, both natural and social, must be *forgotten* by its citizens. The forgetting process is, historically, racial – as always, each type of death noted here attracted widespread media and conversational coverage precisely because, for a change, all the victims were white. Even so, projecting white terrors on to Aborigines is not enough. Hence, the first thing needful now is not facts but ignorance; an economy that produces ignorance of what is all too well known, in favour of new knowledges, ignorances that bring the possibility of comfort, of coherence, even of survival. A part of the economy of ignorance is the America's Cup.

A ritual of locomotion

Twelve-metre yachts travel at about nine miles an hour. The difference between the best in the world and the also-rans – each with its twenty-million-dollar budget, computer-enhanced design and tactics, and its three-year development programme using, in Conner's case at least, facilities normally associated not with sporting but with military hardware – is about one-twentieth of a knot.

Western Australia is a laboratory of locomotion; distance, heat, time, space, and isolation exert their tyrannous imperatives. To get in, to get out, to get around – these are all *hard*. It was only as the Cup's preliminary races were getting under way off Fremantle that, in September 1986, bitumen was laid on the road from Fitzroy Crossing to Hall's Creek, completing the biggest civil-engineering project ever undertaken in Australia, a sealed 'ring road' right round the continent.

To make a 30-tonne yacht travel at one-twentieth of a knot faster than others – this too is *hard*. And, like a strip of bitumen just wide enough to allow two road-trains to pass, it is not by itself very spectacular. But bitumen, travel, and speed are manifestations of – if it has one – the essence of modernity, namely mobility:

> In recent decades, mobility has exploded to the point of characterizing everyday life much more than the traditional image of the 'home and family'. Transport ceases to function as a metaphor of progress or at least of 'modern' life, and becomes instead the primary activity of existence.[5]

The America's Cup is a ritual of locomotion, a spectacular, euphoric, historic, nationalistic, excessive performance of the ability to transgress the laws of space/time, to dissolve the distinctions between here/now and there/then. It celebrates the achievement of the modern military-industrial democracies – to *mobilize* their citizens. Now it's no longer travel *to*, travel *through*, or travel *for*; it's just travel, emancipated from destination or mere functional utility. Paradoxically, to travel: an *intransitive* verb. And mobility excites not just the bodies of the citizens but meanings too: there is mobility of signification. Organized around the familiar fictions of sporting, corporate, and political competition, the America's Cup is not just two boats and two syndicates sailing, spending, and slogging their way slowly to victory. It is a ritual of locomotion, in which the supplementary aspects take precedence over the supposed primary event (which no one can see clearly in any case, except on television). In and around Fremantle the old-fashioned, titanic struggle of the age of realism, between the icy truth of actuality and the vainglorious falsehood of media hype, is simply superseded. The traditional course of events is inverted; actuality becomes a media production.

In a spectacular performance of photogenia, and in the service of the new media science of global euphorics, all possible modes of transport congregate in, off, and above Fremantle, to participate in the ritual, to be there, to be photographed.[6] Many of them already enjoy celebrity status as media stars, besides their spectacularity as visual confirmation of the age of mobility. In pride of place are the liners, reminders of pioneering, epic, luxurious, dangerous transport. There's the *Achille Lauro*, star of spectacular, terrorist politics; one of P & O's *Princesses*, star of TV's *Love Boat* (which was timed to arrive for the final but missed it by a day because *Kookaburra III* went down 'four–zip' to *Stars and Stripes*, instead of forcing Conner to the best of seven races); and there are a couple of Cunarders. There's *The Bounty*, star of the eponymous film and ready for its trip to Portsmouth, to become the flagship of the First Fleet Re-Enactment for Australia's bicentennial celebration. The USS *Missouri* stops by, to remind everyone what real warships look like, and recalling the day when the Second World War was brought formally to a close at a signing ceremony on board, inaugurating the new post-war era of mass mobility. There's the armada of private luxury boats, from Alan Bond's and the Aga Khan's to John (Foster's lager) Elliott's historic Cardiff-registered *Welsh Falcon*, and unique wonders like the Maori war-canoe imported to enhance the 'Kiwi Magic', or the replica Viking longship built in a shed in the Perth suburb of Myaree, not to mention the giant Japanese cargo ship that sailed straight through one of the races.

Then there are the specially built, converted, or imported floating television sets. Perhaps the most spectacular is the square-rigged barquentine *Leeuwin*, built for the Sail Training Association of WA with the help of a $600,000 donation from local businessman Denis Horgan (whose *Island Hopper* helicopters are another prominent feature of the Cup spectacle). Horgan has chartered the *Leeuwin* for the duration of the Cup and spent a further $300,000 on fitting it out 'to world-class luxury'; 'a solid, warm, clubby sort of feeling. Lots of brass with tan and burgundy upholstery' and 'beautifully detailed European ash joinery'.[7] But all these fittings are to be ripped out after the Cup, along with the many television monitors, one of which is located on deck to allow full integration of actuality and image – real *sensurround*. The spectator fleet also includes the big cats like the *Motive Explorer*, each fitted out with TV sets and running commentary while following the action. Naturally, the *Motive Explorer* has since been renamed the *Kimberley Explorer* and sent off to tour the now-famous waters off the far north-west, along with others like the inappropriately named *That's Life!*, whose newspaper advertisement cheerfully encourages life to follow art, if not death:

You've seen Crocodile Dundee, World Safari and The Wonders of Western Australia, now experience the excitement and exhilaration of our 'wild north' first hand! Sail north from Broome to mighty Prince Regent River on magnificent 'That's Life!' From $982.

Naturally, the ad graces the TV page of the *Western Mail*'s colour magazine, and features a photo of the very spot where – as everyone remembers – crocodiles lurk, waiting for unsuspecting tourists . . .

Not only at sea, but also on land and in the air, the transportation flocks. Jumbos luxuriate at Perth's new international air terminal, helicopters throng Fremantle's new heliport, the little ones dancing above the regatta, occasionally towing the biggest Australian flag you ever saw, the big ones clattering across to Rottnest, holiday island. And, lumbering over them all, the anachronistic Bond airship, futuristic high-tech retro throwback, flagship for and constant visual reminder of its ubiquitous, tubby, friendly owner. Naturally, it advertises Swan Premium lager, stylishly outshining the noisy little mono- and biplanes which hawk their way up and down the beaches, towing advertising banners until the final day, when an enthusiastic but over-hasty message is unfurled: 'CONGRATULATIONS STARS AND STRIPS' (*sic*).

On the ground, transportation intensifies. The roads are signposted 'THIS IS A COMMONWEALTH FUNDED AMERICA'S CUP PROJECT'. On them scurry white push-bikes, rented out to advertise Radio 6PR, and you can also rent mopeds (an allusion to Eileen Bond's favoured mode of transport), or Mini Mokes, last seen on television's classic series, *The Prisoner*. *The Prisoner* was filmed in the Welsh 'town' of Portmeirion, a virtually full-scale architectural folly or *trompe-l'œil* designed to look like a Mediterranean city. Fremantle is perhaps the first example of the 'Portmeirionization' of an existing city, though opinions differ on whether its pastel colours are quoting the Mediterranean or *Miami Vice*. But, if you don't see yourself as Danger Man, then there's the tram, specially created, there's the stretched limo service, the Hotham Valley Railway on the 'Spinnaker Run' through Fremantle by real coal-fired steam-engine, there are the 400 extra taxis, or you can even buy a limited-edition 'Challenge' version of a family sedan. There's a jocular hymn to free enterprise, popular culture, and engineering: the longest Cadillac in the world, complete with unlikely fittings including swimming pool, cinema, helipad, and bedroom. Its spectacularity is too excessive, however, for it to appear on the streets – you have to pay $2 and cram into a little marquee on the Esplanade to see it, before crossing the green for refreshments at the converted railway-carriage snack-bar. And among it all, crocodilian, lurks the biggest force of traffic cops ever assembled in WA, ready to enforce the law's dim view of spectacular behaviour and (chemically induced) euphoria.

Perth's cup floweth over when, it glimpses *en route* from kissed airport tarmac to Ascot racecourse, the vehicle that is a mode of transport by itself, the ultimate in uniqueness and spectacularity, the Popemobile.

The challenge

From the state government's point of view, the point of view of surveillance, the population of the land mass known as Western Australia is not to be trusted; it displays a disorganized gaze, a lack of bodily integrity, a need for now the bearer of other, olfactory realities. Day and night, the otherwise empty Commonwealth-Funded America's Cup streets reverberated to the sound of trucks laden with hundreds of thousands of live sheep, to be herded on to strange, Beirut-registered ships with twelve-storey superstructures to house the animals on their way to an exotic death in Libya. As the smell of shit pervades the city, the citizens are reminded just how close they are, from the point of view of the state, to sheep.

To official eyes, then, the population of Western Australia are not yet people. They are bits of people – eyes, ears, noses. They are bodies, to be put into the time and space deemed fit for them. They are bodily functions, to be protected from the accidental discovery that life is sexually transmitted. In short, the people are merely one more example of the primary produce for which Western Australia is so justly famous; they are raw materials.

The challenge, however, is not just to extract this material from the hole in the ground, as is customary in Western Australia, but to transform it – from nature to culture, from bits and pieces into a complex, fully functioning product, from immobility to self-sustaining activity, from raw materials to surplus value. That is, those gazes, times, sounds, movements, and functions have to be made into people. And those people have to be made into a community. This is a challenge which the state is content to leave to others – specifically, to television.

The politics of euphoria

The Challenge – is it a car? Is it a race? Is it a harbour? Well, yes, but it's also a mini-series. Broadcast on Alan Bond's Channel Nine in Perth, sponsored by Alan Bond's Swan Premium lager, it is about Alan Bond's successful challenge for the America's Cup in 1983, and, for all we know, Alan Bond is watching it with Eileen, hoping it will psych the visiting syndicates for the 1987 challenge who are no doubt watching it too. The imagined community of Western Australia is united around the figure of Alan Bond, dissolving the distinction between reality and fiction, engaging the audience's gaze, organizing sights and sounds into an economy of coherence by means of audio-visual excitement, a pedagogic and seductive regime of pleasure within which there are multiple spectator positions, but every one of them is OK by Bondy. Look up! It's Bondy's airship, and it's his tower that pierces skywards over Perth. Now he plans another in Sydney, the tallest building in the southern hemisphere, 114 metres taller than the Centrepoint Tower. Look there! It's Bondy's coal mine, gold mine. Look here! It's Bondy's TV station, brewery, hotel, 12-metre yacht, private university . . .

Not only has he got the local consciousness industries sown up, but Alan Bond personifies their myths. He arrived in Fremantle on the P & O liner *Himalaya* aged 13, took his first job as a signwriter, and had a hand in painting the giant red dingo that adorns the side of the flour mill overlooking the America's Cup course off North Fremantle. An epitome of social mobility, he's the ambiguation of opposites – worker capitalist, popular rich man, 'our' Bondy whose corporation operates globally. And he's ready to discipline. However, during the Cup, the authorities averted their eyes and handed the people over to the media, to be recruited, mobilized, into acting as the cast of thousands, extras in the performance of modernity. Their gaze was deregulated, privatized, their bodies let loose, their spaces, sounds, times, and movements were untrammelled. Of course, this was countenanced mainly to impress the visitors from over east and overseas, to flatter them with the idea that Western Australia isn't a parochial backwater but a teeming, colourful image of their expectations of it – a flattery which also declared that Western Australians haven't really got an identity of their own, but exist only as products of the visitors' perceptions, figments of the foreign imagination.

After the Cup, in defeat, the people were required to delegate their desires back to the state and local government, to submit to the former regime of untrustworthiness in which the authorities decide where and at what they can look. Hotels were forced to ban the strip and lingerie shows that had proliferated during the Cup. Drive-in movie theatres were threatened, because pictures were spilling out of the confines of the car parks into the windows of the neighbours, and some of those pictures were sexy. The new and proposed buildings in Perth's central business district were judged to be too exuberant, and in need of regulating down to a height commensurate with the horizons of the planning minister's imagination. And constabulary boots tramped laboriously across the sands of the city's beaches, putting a stop to topless sunbathing – an illegal practice (for women) to which the authorities had turned a blind eye during the Cup.

The people's gaze was reorganized, directed, made respectable once more. But, once invoked, rights cannot be revoked with impunity. Now people displayed mobility of another kind, by voting on the new regime with their feet: they deserted not just the hotels, drive-ins, and beaches, but the city and the streets as well. In an attempt to win them back, Perth City Council could think of nothing better than to regulate their hearing. It banned buskers from the city centre during peak hours, so that shoppers wouldn't be distracted from single-minded concentration on their civic duty to enter shops and spend money. During the Cup, shopping had been promoted not as a duty but as a pleasure; for the first time stores had been allowed to stay open on Saturday afternoons. Now they were forced to shut again, so there was little time to waste on pleasurable congregation, assuming people had managed to outwit the government's bizarre revenge on modernity – to build a city that absolutely requires you to get about by car and then closes virtually all the petrol stations in the evenings and over the weekend. These impediments to mobility and regulations of time were such that it didn't matter that the pubs were forced to close earlier too, since no one was left on the streets to notice.

As if to confirm their power over people's senses, the powers-that-be celebrated the end of the Cup with a reminder to the citizens of Fremantle that their city's primary purpose and function was to serve as a conduit, removing the produce that primary industry had managed to scrape from the surface of the land. The famous Fremantle Doctor, the breeze that had so recently carried Dennis Conner to victory and the Cup to San Diego, was supply the American's Cup 1987 with its crowning *coup de théâtre*. On losing 'his' cup, he doesn't whinge or weep; he celebrates: buying Kerry Packer's broadcasting interests, selling his yachts to the Japanese (apart from *Australia II*, which has already been acquired by the Commonwealth as a national treasure), and so turning, overnight, from Australia's biggest brewer into Australia's biggest media baron as well. Mythic magic – in Perth he's known as 'Crocodile Bondee', at least on T-shirts.

But his power isn't just purchasing power, it's the power of mobilization, and it's not Bond's personal power but the power of what he personifies: the power of television. It converts a city into a set, people into performers, and it commands the presence here in Perth of the world's finest, stars of actuality. Appropriately, in a secular equivalent of the papal visit, the presence here of the world's media is symbolized by the arrival of Walter Cronkite and Princess Anne – if it has any, the essences of broadcasting and its subject. The excitement, euphoria, and activity generated during the Cup were there for the taking, emancipating Perth from the horrors and barbarities that lurk so close, and plugging it in, momentarily, to the global economy of surplus meaning that induces forgetfulness of the confines of regulated routine, and reminds the people of the possibilities (as yet unrealized) of new freedoms, of movement, of choice, of pleasure.

In the end, then, the power of television is to mobilize the citizens of military-industrial democracies in ways that official authorities seem not only unable to match, but actively to resent. However, the presence of the genial Prime Minister of Australia, strolling the sunny streets of the Fremantle set after officially unfurling yet another gigantic Australian flag over the Roundhouse, WA's oldest building and first prison, suggests that the higher levels of government, at least, understand only too well the need to unify the people into an imagined community of citizens who can be mobilized to see themselves as free to choose in the name not of ideology but of euphoria. In the new age of signs without referents, of media-produced reality, of pedagogic seduction, the people can make sense of democracy as competition; they can understand economics, politics, and social structure in terms of sport – no longer the sport of kings but of transnational corporations and their 'barons'; they can become in the end what the media hype required of them: The People, ultimate fiction, stars of the show, who exercise their historic right to join the party by partying.

A pity for the nearly-nation of Western Australia, if not for its newly appointed 'ambassador', Dennis Conner, the party's over.[8]

Murdoch University, Western Australia

Notes

1 Exemplified most recently by the opening of what should prove to be the world's largest iron ore mine, aptly named McCamey's Monster.

2 See Martyn Webb, 'Regionalization and the making of Western Australia', paper presented at the Imaging Western Australia symposium, April 1987, and deposited in the J. S. Battye Library of Western Australian History, Perth.
3 The reference is now not confined to Joseph Conrad's nineteenth-century invocation of white terror, but extends, interestingly, to Francis Ford Coppola's contemporary version of it, *Apocalypse Now*.
4 Thomas Hardy, 'The convergence of the twain (lines on the loss of the *Titanic*)', in *The Collected Poems of Thomas Hardy*, 4th edn (London: Macmillan, 1930), pp. 288–9.
5 Paolo Prato and Gianluca Trivero, 'The spectacle of travel', *Australian Journal of Cultural Studies*, 3, 2 (1985), pp. 25–43.
6 The photogenia of the event is perhaps gauged by the estimated consumption in the America's Cup Media Centre of 36,550 sheets of monochrome print paper per month and 20,000 rolls of film per month during the five months of the Cup. See *The Western Mail Magazine*, 27 September 1986, p. 38.
7 Ibid., p. 14.
8 Several months later, the euphoria having been killed off, a competition in the local papers revealed some popular images of WA. 14,420 suggestions for a new slogan for the State's vehicle licence plates. Leading suggestions were *The Friendly State* (which received most nominations), *The Great State*, *The State For All Seasons*, *The Wildflower State*. Unlikely, but revealing, were *Smoking – No WA* and *WA – Beer Bull & Brawl*. There was in fact an overwhelming majority against the offically chosen 'winner'. WA – THE GOLDEN STATE. However, this regression to the hole in the ground was appropriately rewarded – the competition winner received a half 'Nugget', the new, ideologically sound Australian version of the Krugerrand made from gold extracted, naturally, from Western Australia.

TONY FRY AND

ANNE-MARIE WILLIS

EXPO 88: BACKWOODS INTO THE FUTURE

E xpo 88 is a world event on the edge of several worlds. In trying to make the city of Brisbane visible to 'the world', it has achieved almost total invisibility. While aiming to attain international status, it has managed, through its limited visions and lack of originality, only to reinforce and reproduce the economic, cultural, and political marginality not only of Brisbane but of the Australian nation within a world order.

Some thirty nine countries have signed up to participate in Expo 88, which is to be held on the banks of the Brisbane River during Australia's bicentennial year. Displays will address the theme of 'Leisure in the Age of Technology'. Some of the large corporate participants are IBM, Ford, Qantas, and Fuji. Participating nations fall into several categories: major economic powers (Japan, the USA, Germany), near neighbours (New Zealand, Papua New Guinea, Fiji, Tonga), and a large group of very small nations which, like the state of Queensland and Australia itself, are becomingly increasingly economically dependent on tourism (Nepal, the Seychelles, Dominica).

Expo 88 is an echo of previous world expositions, it is a site for the fallout of narratives of modernity, so in looking forward it looks backwards. But there are ways in which it does unknowingly look future-ward, prefiguring new patterns of restructuring within the world order. It is symptomatic and prefigurative of the cultural economy of spectacularization, most particularly in the arena of increasingly commodified, totally packaged, and highly organized forms of leisure, in which leisure products and service relations are articulated in geo-spatial, social, economic, and political orders of development and underdevelopment.

As we count down the months to go before the opening, controversy rages, underlining the fact that Expo 88 has always existed in a precarious state. The Federal government showed little interest until recently offered substantial concessions and the Labor states, the 'enemies' of Queensland National Party ex-Premier Bjelke-Petersen, are refusing to participate. Brisbane hotel industry representatives are concerned about the lack of expected advance bookings for this claimed 'international' event. A report prepared by Ron Woodall, Creative Director of the successful Vancouver Expo 86, points to inadequate funding, lack of overseas promotion, and, most significantly, a lack of creative design and theme development, without which Expo 88 will fail as an international event.[1]

Expo 88 is located on a 40-hectare site opposite the central business district, but separated from it by the river. This prime piece of real estate, the original site of the old city of Brisbane, has been cleared of its former waterfront and light-industrial activities. An Expo press release describes this as an act of 'converting an underdeveloped section of river frontage into a futuristic masterpiece of architectural design'. This is not how the people of adjacent communities view Expo. What resident action groups have pointed to is the event's negative effects – increased traffic and parking problems, and heightened demand for property by business and tourism, which will increase rents, rates, and purchase prices, and which will add up to a (mis)managed social transformation of the area. People didn't have to wait until 1988 for such things to happen. Two boarding-houses which had provided low-cost accommodation for predominantly Aboriginal people, one of these being the first Aboriginal hostel to have been established in Brisbane, have been demolished. New roads and traffic systems, along with the disruptions to local life caused by a major building site, have already brought Expo into the present for many people.[2] Expo has made its mark on Brisbane in other ways: people are now living with an artificial lagoon, a fibreglass mountain, and a permanent Disneyland-type amusement park. And with the site's seven tension-membrane canopies Expo has become a highly visible *sign* to the city's inhabitants.

Our purpose is not to try to predict the final form of the event, or to write a local history, or to examine it as a set of activities occurring on a bounded site. Even if it were to be cancelled tomorrow, Expo has already had a material existence: it is a national political issue; it is a site on the banks of the Brisbane River on which buildings have been demolished and others built, communities have been displaced, an old micro-economy is being phased out while another is in the process of being phased in, real-estate values have altered, some people have lost jobs and others have gained them. Additionally, resident action groups spent months mounting campaigns in opposition. So 'the event' has changed thousands of lives, and all of this before 'the event' itself has happened. It is an event which has its most immediate echoes in Brisbane itself, particularly as a cause of political wrangling. This micro-politics, however, will not be our concern. What we are going to do is to offer a number of different kinds of symptomatic and critical readings of Expo. What we shall actually look at will be:

1 Expo as a historical placement – as a concept, as a teleology (a progression of Expos), and as a location in a particular national/international configuration of space and power.
2 Expo as an imaginary representation – that which is designed as the specification of that which will be built (here we use design beyond the

limits of appearances), as well as what the planners *think* that they are bringing into being (the notion of *theme* being a key here). Within this area of reading, the event will be engaged using the notion of operational discourse.

In viewing the event in such ways, we are adopting a mode of criticism which is both non-reductive and potentially interventionist. There is no fixed, open, closed, or fully authored phenomenological text before us, but there are numerous textual processes and effects. By undertaking this kind of criticism, we are *de facto* aiming at the manufacture of the production of historio-political readings which pre-date the finished production of the text by its authors. This is to say that the *process* of authorship at the time of production comes within the orbit of criticism. When a project's objective is representational, such a critical practice could generate transformatory dialogue or polemic. Architectural criticism is one clear arena where such interventionist strategies have a prehistory, for example in campaigns of objection to proposed building or demolition. As corporate clients invest more and more in buying 'good taste', critical interventions before purchase or public exposure can effect changes in client and public reading, attitude, and comment. Criticism thus can have the potential to recode prior to the completion of encoding.

The space of history

We can, and need to, place Expo 88 in time and historically constituted space in a number of ways – as a fragmented temporal text of multiple forms; as an Expo among Expos; as a historical exposure; and as object-event in a particular location (Brisbane, Queensland, Australia). Each of these placements will be taken in turn.

A FRAGMENT OF THE HERE AND NOW

The multiplicity of Expo 88 can partly be understood as a variety of voices which speak through it, as a plurality of aesthetic forms within the total design, as a moment of formation at the time of writing or reading this text, or as a moment or moments of representational encounter. All of this is to say that as a text object it is non-synchronic. However, such an observation should be extended further.

For this 'original event' the dominant visual form – the sail-like structures of its seven pavilions – is twenty years old. The tent-roof constructions designed by Frei Otto for the Pavilion of the Federal Republic of Germany at the Montreal Expo of 1967 were almost exactly the same as the Brisbane structures. So, as a skyline form of the future, it has the look of the unmodified past. At the same time as looking like a projection from the past, Expo 88 is also displaced in its projected claims to represent forms of the future before they exist. It was a past even before being encountered as a present. For, by the end of 1986, the design for Expo 92 had been decided.

Architect Emilio Ambasz had won the prize for the 'master plan' of the exhibition to celebrate the 500th anniversary of Columbus's 'discovery' of America (the finding of another never lost land), to take place in Seville, Spain. The design itself is predicated upon the design of post-Expo use of the site as the rationale for the concept.

A TELLING TELEOLOGY – AN EXPO AMONG EXPOS

Expo 88 casts itself, via the hands of its organizers, in the context of major world expositions that began with the Great Exhibition of 1851 in London. From the exhibits of the halls of the Crystal Palace to perhaps Montreal in 1967, all world expositions were celebrations and advocations of modernity – the spirit, form, and products of a society of mass production and consumption. Of course, the lineage is a retrospective construct; the relation between one event and the other (Paris, 1867, 1878, 1889, 1927; Philadelphia, 1876; St Louis, 1904; San Francisco, 1915; New York, 1939; Brussels, 1858; Montreal, 1967; Osaka, 1970 – these are just some from a listing) is a product of the historian rather than a planned history that every organizing committee agreed upon and worked to contribute to. The very listing of events which should be included is open to contestation. One nation's major event is another nation's minor commitment. The status of these expositions is very variable and clearly subject to values held at the point of assessment.

From 1967 onwards, the celebration of modernity as the common, if unstated, subtext of the narrative of every Expo starts to look shaky. By then the crisis of modernity, as a master narrative of progress, begins to break up or perhaps down. Habitat 67 (the theme title at Montreal) engaged urban life, contemplated the city of the future, and explored innovation in built environments. At the same time, by implication, its theme acknowledged a crisis of modern life. Explicitly the nature and speed of the development of modern cities were addressed. The dichotomy between modernity as progress and modernity as crisis has been in place ever since – The Environment (Spokane, 1974), Energy (Knoxville, 1982), Transport (Vancouver, 1986) are confirmatory examples. Brisbane, whether its organizers know it or not, is no exception to this. To link leisure and technology as theme is to signal an area of neo-capitalist development. It also marks hyper-capitalism and post-industrial crisis, especially in the further colonization of our imaginations and increased unevenness of uneven development.

In comparative terms of historical significance, scale, capital investment, geographic location (in relation to centres of metropolitan neo-capitalist development), concept, form, and some of its content, Expo 88 is marginal. The nature of this marginality will be commented upon in a moment, but first we want to reconnect with our earlier comments on criticism.

If marginality has a psychology – and we would argue that it does – then inherent in it is a deference to the authority of the elsewhere. For marginal economies, such events as expositions are implicated in the discourse of development. They are, for countries like Australia, the production of sites for self-representation of belonging to the dominant world order; of impressing eyes from elsewhere; and of expressions of confidence to feed self-image and images of self. All of these manifestations of the marginal mentality make such events and their representations vulnerable to the kind of criticism which could recode them for investors and visitors, especially influential ones. This reaffirms our earlier comments on the value of such strategic criticism. In addition, the secret modes of operation, the paranoid reactions to questions about the Expo authority, the infighting between the political game-callers and brought-in experts, as well as the 'cleaning up' of the area (which mainly means shipping the Aboriginal dispossessed out of a nearby park, where they live – to ensure that the protests of the 1981 Commonwealth Games over land rights do not happen again), all support claims about the insecurity of promoted 'local' constructions of modernizing progressive spaces, forces, and forms. There is no local hegemony of progress, a consensus has not been won, and double-dealing substitutes for coercion.

EXPOSURES OF EXPO

The very word 'exposition' suggests an event in or at which there is something to expose or to exposit. At the height of this form of spectacle, inseparable from the peak of an optimistic modernity, there was a sense of the significance of the exhibition form and function. National political, economic, and cultural leaders around the world worked with such assumptions – the wonders of art, industry, science, and technology were to be marvelled at, 'the people' had to be educated, and progress had to be celebrated. There was almost a sense of urgency, for instance, at the Great Exhibition of 1851, a sense of necessity to reveal the wonders of industrialization and the fruits of colonialism to a public in order to strive to colonize people's imaginations with narratives of progress and faith in Empire. International expositions have historically been a means for the induction of public consciousness into the economic and cultural projects that were already transforming their lives. They attempted to make sense of the dislocation, fragmentation, and bewildering changes people were experiencing in their daily lives, by installing overarching narratives that papered over contradictions and painted a picture of a forward march of civilization powered by technological innovation and scientific rationality.

With faith in that kind of modernity shattered, the rejection of that narrative provided the urgent message to be 'exposed', which was the logic of the major post-1967 Expos (as we have seen). The organizers of Expo 88 would seem to be unaware of this shift, as is evidenced by their uncritical coupling of leisure and technology. But, perhaps more significantly, what is missing from Expo 88 is a belief that there is something urgent to expose/exposit. There is no sense that any narrative is being constructed with a new message, designed to inspire, to capture imaginations. It is an event looking for an idea rather than the reverse. Where once a theme had substance, was content-laden, it has now become a representational device which invites much scratching of heads and anguish in the search for inspiration. This, as we shall now see, is completely consistent with the political regime that is responsible for Expo 88.

THE PLACE OF THE OBJECT-EVENT

Expo is both the effect of the echo and a means of its production; the intention is to signify to the world, the nation, and the local area that the 'international', in the form of the appearance of advanced modernity, has arrived.

Brisbane is on the margins of the margins, and so too is the state of Queensland. Marginality in this kind of usage defines a complex series of cultural, economic, and social relations. Australia is on the edge of the developed world; it is a *de facto* client state of capitalism.[3] The nation represents itself as a free and advanced nation. This is a façade. It is dependent upon the fate of markets and other forces elsewhere for both the sale of its extractive-industry primary products (which are mainly taken out of the ground by foreign-owned mining companies) and for imports of products that its limited manufacturing base is unable to produce economically. Cultural norms, recognition, markets, centres of excellence, and so on, are located elsewhere; therefore, however good 'the local' may be, it is either in the wings of the world stage or, if spotlighted, illuminated somewhere else. Australia has a small population and a great deal of empty space. People live on its edge, and that edge is on no one's route to anywhere. The cultural fringe is not just the consequence of a fringe history; it is also a product of a Euro-American ethnocentrism of objects and agendas (of what is proper, serious, valued, etc.) operating in the psychology of marginality.

As indicated, there are relative positions of marginality within marginal Australia. While this can be, and is, figured as distance of location to the metropolitan centres of Melbourne and Sydney, and the economic and political power of Victoria and New South Wales, it should not be seen as exclusively geo-spatial. The Aboriginal peoples of Australia, the fringe dwellers on the fringe, occupy this marginality – be they leading a tribal life in the empty centre or living in the anomie of urban poverty. Either way, these people have no political, cultural, or economic power. Hence the very character of practised resistance is, literally and metaphorically, hit-and-run skirmishing, the past way of waging war in the culture translated and transmuted into the present.

International expositions are generally awarded to nations and host cities, and although Expo 88 has been awarded by the international committee to Australia, with Brisbane as the host city, the Federal government transferred the power to organize and stage Expo 88 to the Queensland government, which then set up an independent Expo authority. This arrangement evidences the fragmented nature and history of contradiction and conflict within Australia's political system, in which individual states retain powers in a number of areas and consistently seek to assert their concerns over the

Federal government. The controversies and wranglings over Expo are evidence of dysfunctionality at a structural level. Having transferred responsibility for Expo to Queensland, the Federal government showed a lack of commitment until late in the project's development. This has been evident even outside the country, with international criticisms of the paltry funds allocated to developing countries who wish to exhibit.[4] This failure to take the exercise seriously can partly be explained by the hostility that exists between the Federal Labor government and the National-Party-led government of Queensland, for, if Expo were to be a success, the perception is that the aggressively reactionary (now ex-), Premier of Queensland, Sir Joh Bjelke-Petersen, would take all the credit. This is also partly why the (Labor) governments of New South Wales, Victoria, South Australia, and Western Australia were reluctant to participate.[5]

The Queensland government has got behind Expo wholeheartedly. It fits their bill as an ideal project to give a focus to the regime's desired image of economic advancement within a frame of old-style modernity. This is needed with particular urgency in the context of the state's poor national image, especially in relation to corruption. The hope is that Expo will both publicize on an international level and provide a boost to the fast-developing tourist economy of Queensland. This form of economic activity is being increasingly promoted, in the face of the decline in agribusiness.

Ambitious claims have been made by the Expo 88 authority. The most notable is that the event will attract eight million visitors and a huge influx of international tourists, many of whom, it is hoped, will travel beyond Brisbane to spend their tourist dollars in the burgeoning coastal and Barrier Reef island resorts. Such projections are used to sustain the Queensland governments's claims that it has the key to the nation's economic future.

The racist policies and practices of the Queensland government are notorious. The Aboriginal population of 50,000 forms a forgotten underclass only marginally integrated into the economy and totally invisible in official discourses of progress and prosperity. For example, in an illustrated booklet, *Queensland Australia*, produced by the Premier's department for international distribution, not one image of an Aboriginal person appears; Aboriginal issues, except for integrationist 'success stories', are rare in the mainstream media; and, while Aboriginal people, still living under a semi-apartheid system, have little to gain from the growth of tourism, their traditional culture, in the form of rock paintings and artefacts, is presented as a spectacularized 'primitive' by the tourist industry, thus rendering contemporary Aboriginal culture invisible and positioning Aboriginals as people of the past, not as people with a future.[6]

With the increasing emphasis on the development of tourism in a framework of free enterprise, Aboriginal people are likely to lose out all round. Expensive restaurants line the waterfront esplanade of the tropical city of Cairns. While American and Japanese tourists dine on lobster and coral trout, they can look out on groups of Aboriginals and Torres Strait Islanders congregating along the waterfront park, while a police car cruises down the esplanade shining a torch to survey their behaviour. It is not simply 'unruly' behaviour that is being policed, but the boundaries of Aboriginality; for Aboriginality is not permitted an urban twentieth-century existence in Queensland. In towns and cities, it is to be either assimilated out of existence or, within the discourses of tourism, allowed only a museumified and commodified presence as spectacle of the past.

The manner in which the decision to stage Expo 88 was made is symptomatic of the working of the Queensland political system. The decision was made in secrecy, with no parliamentary debate or prior consultation with the communities to be affected. There was no public acknowledgement of, or even replies made to, the hundreds of letters of objection sent to the Expo authority and the various government departments concerned.[7]

Exploitations: imaginaries and effects

Investment in Expo 88 by the Federal and Queensland governments, the city of Brisbane, and overseas and Australian corporations is all predicated upon its having various effects – some of which we have already indicated as the desires of the participants. As a site of the production of the sign, the event needs to be understood: as a prefiguration (a name to speak and act upon as a means to author(ize) change); as a sign in a pattern of planned progress which is a part of a meta-object – a new Brisbane; as a deployment of theme-ing; and as an after-event (many of the prefigurations can be seen to have been aimed at post-event effects, for example the revaluing of real estate). We shall not expand prefigurations further. The remaining ways of examining sign production and deployment will be commented upon. First, however, it is important to pick up on earlier references to the multiplicity of the event. While this is the case, there is a use of representation to counter this perception – by the application of the name 'Expo 88', by its visual identity, and by the function of theme-ing. However, more needs to be claimed than this, for, as is becoming clearer, a great deal is being and will be done in the name of Expo. Its exercise, dispersals, and flows of power in fact define it as an *operational discourse*. What we mean by this is a discourse which is instrumentally employed in the mobilization of narratives of appearance and authority (which in the case in question is dominated by the narrative *intention* of theme-ing) for empowering effectivities of event difference characterized by the different functioning of forms, practices, effects. The objective of operational discourse, as a directional force which never totally directs, is to take up subjects and move them through a preferred, or ensembles of preferred, readings/actions.[8] Unlike narrative structure, operational discourse does not rest upon sequential progressions, narratives, or a monadic text.

A SIGN OF PLANNED PROGRESS

To understand Expo 88 within this remit is, as has been said, to look at it as part of the meta-object of a new Brisbane, or rather the desire to represent

Brisbane as new. The generative centre of the restructuring of Brisbane's image and economy is the Eagle and Creek Street area. This new finance-capital heartland has an overt politics of representation. It is populated by corporations making heavy investments in a late-modern look, in terms of architecture, interior design, graphic design, and all the other means of constituting corporate culture and extending corporate identities. Since it is regarded as the leading edge of the appearance of development in the city and beyond, as a major source of development finance, and as the backers of new service industries, especially tourism, there is a recognition that the image of Brisbane/Queensland has exchange value. This is as developable real estate and as a purchasable image of desire. It follows, then, that the recognition sought by Expo 88 and the credibility it desires is subordinate to serving a more deeply embedded new power-base of the city, as well as the established local political old guard.

ON THEME-ING

The basic premise for the application of theme-ing is a representational strategy which, for expediency's sake, sets out to construct appearances of unity and coherence where there is no narrativity or continuity. Commodity theme-ing not only fails to acknowledge arbitrariness and contradiction (that is, difference); it actively aims to conceal.

The theme of Expo 88 is the problematic figure of leisure.[9] It set out to provide and promote this theme as a viable package to harmonize the difference of the broad spectrum of contributors it hoped would participate. As a pluralistic concept, it was also deemed to be open to different definitions and inflections by the nations and corporations that buy into the project. The Expo authority has been heavily criticized for poor 'theme management' – it is regarded as having been so loose as to fail to cohere anything. Without a functioning theme, the operational discourse is rendered partly dysfunctional.

Leisure is meant to imply a mixture of high-tech spin-off, progress, and new pleasure options. A linking of leisure and technology in Expo's theme is intended to usher in a 'commonsense' notion that technology can provide the means for work to be done for 'society', thus making more time available for leisure. Once a utopian vision, now no longer tenable, the reality of high-tech industry and automation is now here, and the effects – those of long-term structural unemployment in both First and Third Worlds – are distressingly familiar. Expo 88 is not concerned with this enforced leisure, for the 'leisure' of the unemployed cannot be harnessed to the generation of profits. By optimistically linking leisure and technology, then, Expo 88 addresses leisure entirely within the context of the developing end of uneven development and the specific expansion of corporate culture. Increased leisure time produced by technology is of benefit only to those classes that can profit by it.

Yet the official rhetoric speaks of leisure as 'a concept of universal understanding with no cultural or socio-economic barriers'![10] Such a statement echoes the universalist tone of modernity which, as we have mentioned, has underwritten all major expositions. Nevertheless, this particular façade of equality and unity has its own specificity:

> Leisure as a Universal Pastime will give exhibitors the opportunity to comprehensively demonstrate the range of leisure pursuits available in their individual countries. It will also encourage cultural exchange and highlight the countries' primary tourist attractions.[11]

Such impoverished aspirations can be seen to be opportunistically related to Queensland's concern with its own tourist economy. It also, significantly, reduces that which is cast as leisure to that which can be purchased by a tourist; this would presumably include customs and traditions within particular cultures which get redesignated as leisure – spectacles for the tourist. Expo thus plans to present simulations of 'culture' several times removed from sources, and to present commodified representations (displays, videos, audio-visuals) of representations that have been created for the gaze of the affluent and mobile consumers of advanced capitalism.

Leisure echoes through the Expo event and beyond. The structure of such an event itself is paradigmatic of managed, packaged, commodified, spectacularized leisure. What kind of leisure experience, then, does Expo 88 offer? It is a family day out, an anticipated 'treat' for children, a group outing for teenagers, a social event, a space–time (among many) in which social interrelations are made. It has a price, and there is limited time for this price, with one-day, three-day, and season tickets available. This puts visitors under pressure to see and do as much as possible, to get maximum 'value for money', and thus plan the number and order of their activities in the framework of the amount of time purchased. So leisure becomes work, and also a source of potential frustration (and family or group conflict!), as each visitor intent on his or her particular route through Expo has to compete with others for access to discrete displays and events. In anticipation of planned crowds and hoped-for long queues (visitors waited up to three and a half hours to gain entry to the popular General Motors pavilion at Expo 86 in Vancouver), Expo 88 will feature roving circus entertainers. Such congestion time is aimed for, as it is aimed to be taken up with visitors buying fast food and souvenirs, which will be presented in multinational theme-nodules across the site and sixteen merchandising pavilions which will be 'easily distinguishable by their interesting roof lines'.[12]

Although pre-event publicity emphasizes that there will be plenty of active displays at Expo 88, things to do as well as to see, the gaze will be dominant, visitors will be primarily placed so as passively to consume spectacles of national and corporate promotion. They will also be the recipients of education and re-education, both in terms of the specific messages conveyed by displays as well as in modes of leisure consumption.

The link between leisure and technology in Expo's theme is clearly problematic. Obvious examples spring to mind: technology is used to produce leisure commodities, high-tech funfair rides, for example. But the technology of the leisure commodity is not exclusive to leisure, not even necessarily designed with leisure use in mind. For example, exactly the same computer hardware can be used for doing office accounts, playing video games, or balancing the household budget. With the uniformity of hardware, software becomes the means of designating and enabling different functions. Work and leisure usage are coded differentially – at the level both of programming and of sign coding (marketing, packaging, advertising, publicity). The same commodity is encoded differently for different markets. This is not simply analogous to the same soft drink being sold under different labels to appeal to different sectors of the market. With computer technology (and this is the technology implied in the theme 'Leisure in the Age of Technology'), it is through coding – that is, the design of both software and the totality of packaging – that actual, functional difference is created.

POST-EXPO 88: THE AFTER-EVENT EVENT

As has been argued throughout this article, part of the aim of Expo 88 for Brisbane's power-brokers is its potential after-effects. What is desired really adds up to the event's co-option in the process of recoding the once 'overgrown country town' as a modern, quasi-postmodern, progressive city. The Expo site, while becoming high-priced real estate after the event, is, more significantly, bound up with and implicated in the construction of a 'space of change' in the service of a city of change. The leisure–technology– pleasure combo plays a tune of changing times. For the more astute speculators on the scene, the spectacle occupies a space to be filled with a new future. For them, Expo 88 was created in order to become a means of displacing a past and to become a past displaced; the operation of the operational discourse thus serves aims beyond the event. For the less astute, Expo 88 was to put Brisbane on the map. In both cases, the hidden agenda of marginality dominates, since marginality works against being taken seriously, gaining respect, having cultural status even when the money rolls in. For all this, so far Brisbane has yet to transcend the glitz of provincial kitsch and the quick-buck deal of the wise guy.

A closing comment

This discussion of Expo 88 is part of a larger project which addresses the political economy of leisure theoretically and across a number of examples in the USA, UK, and Australia. Many of the concepts we have touched on – for example, leisure and operational discourse – are dealt with at greater length in this work.

Of course it is possible to say a great deal more about Expo 88 – we have only brushed on its political economy; appearance (besides its 'look' there is a tale to tell about the parochial control of its design and the failure to make it a national design event); content; its conjunctural moment in the bicentenary year, with all the 'noise' that implies; and its configurations of audience. What, however, we do claim to have signalled is the importance of such events as texts that require critical comment. Furthermore, such comment, as we have argued and now reiterate, is a form of criticism which can be developed to have strategic political importance within a frame which acknowledges the political as a problematic of constant consideration and reconfiguration. It is certainly no longer acceptable to be dismissive of events like Expo 88 as political figures or as cultural forms beneath the 'serious' concerns of critics of high and popular culture or the analysis of 'radical' political economists.

Power Institute of Fine Arts, University of Sydney

Notes

1 For references to the Woodall report and public criticism of Expo 88, see *Times on Sunday* (Sydney), 22 March 1987, 29 March 1987, and 5 April 1987.
2 'Expo 88: why no public debate?', *Black Nation*, 5 (Brisbane, November 1985). Also, our thanks to Ross Watson for giving us information and directing us to material on the anti-Expo activities of the West End Resident Action Group.
3 Greg Crough and Ted Wheelwright, *Australia: A Client State* (Ringwood, Victoria: Penguin, 1982).
4 Sally Loane, 'Expo 88 is shaping up to be a Bicentennial public relations fizzer', *Times on Sunday*, 29 March 1987.
5 The Premiers of South Australia and Western Australia, Mr Burke and Mr Bannon, couched their refusal in terms of economic non-feasibility; see Steve Rous, 'Expo a waste for us: SA, WA Premiers', *The Courier Mail* (Brisbane), 23 December 1986.
6 The Queensland government has been the slowest to dismantle the notorious reserve system; about half the state's Aboriginal population live on these specially designated areas (many are former missions) where they are subject to restrictive laws that do not apply to the rest of the population. For a detailed account of the human-rights injustices encoded into Queensland legislation concerning Aboriginals and Torres Strait Islanders, see Garth Nettheim, *Victims of the Law: Black Queenslanders Today* (Sydney: Allen & Unwin, 1981). Since the publication of this book, some reforms have been introduced, but most operate at the level of appearance and do not involve a genuine transfer of power; an example is the renaming of the Department of Aboriginal and Islander Affairs as the Department of Community Services.
7 *Black Nation*, op. cit.
8 This issue is taken up more fully in our forthcoming book, the working title of which is *Halfway to Paradise: Theme-ing and a Cultural Economy of Leisure*.
9 See note 8.
10 Expo authority press release, no date (1986).
11 Ibid.
12 *World Expo 88 Brisbane* (newsletter), June 1986.
While there are some cosmic reforms by moderates such as Bob Katter Jnr., more blatant forms of oppression continue, a recent example being the decision of Corrective Services Minister Mr Neal to re-open the notorious 'blackhole' cells in Brisbane gaol because of reports of potential aboriginal protests during Expo. *Sydney Morning Herald*, 13 November 1987.

For Product Safety Concerns and Information please contact our EU
representative GPSR@taylorandfrancis.com
Taylor & Francis Verlag GmbH, Kaufingerstraße 24, 80331 München, Germany

www.ingramcontent.com/pod-product-compliance
Lightning Source LLC
Chambersburg PA
CBHW062040270326
41929CB00014B/2481

* 9 7 8 0 4 1 6 0 9 1 5 2 6 *